W9-AKD-269

BARRY LONG, Australian writer and spiritual teacher, was born in 1926 and lives on the Gold Coast of Queensland. His uncompromising and practical approach to the truth of life has attracted an increasing international audience since he began his public teaching in England in 1982.

ONLY FEAR DIES contains eight essays on the causes and effects of unhappiness and the spiritual process of 'dying for life', a way of practical self-knowledge which ultimately brings freedom from fear and liberation from the perpetual discontent of humanity.

Also by Barry Long

Wisdom And Where To Find It
Meditation A Foundation Course
Knowing Yourself
Stillness Is The Way
To Woman In Love

Only
FEAR DIES

A book of liberation

BARRY LONG

 BARRY
LONG
BOOKS

This edition first published 1994
by Barry Long Books
BCM Box 876, London WC1N 3XX England.

Reprinted 1996.

'Only Fear Dies' is a revised and extended edition of 'Ridding Yourself of
Unhappiness', first published by The Barry Long Foundation in 1984.
Three of the essays were originally written to be recorded as audio-tapes:
'The Being Behind The Mask' recorded in 1993 as 'How To Live Joyously';
'The Law of Life' and part of 'Death, Birth and the Secret of Hell' were
recorded in 1985 as 'The Law of Life – Karma'.

© Barry Long 1984, 1993, 1994.

The right of Barry Long to be identified as the author of this work has been
asserted in accordance with sections 77 and 78 of the Copyright Designs
and Patents Act 1988. All rights reserved. No part of this book may be
reproduced, stored in a retrieval system or transmitted in any form or by
any means without the prior permission of the publisher.

Cataloguing-in-Publication Data:
A catalogue record for this book is available from The British Library.
Library of Congress Catalog Card Number: 96-096013.

ISBN 0 9508050 7 6

Cover design: Rene Graphics, Brisbane.
Typesetting: Wordbase Ltd, London.
Photo: International Photographic Library.
Printed in England on acid-free paper by Redwood Books.

BARRY LONG BOOKS are published by The Barry Long Foundation,
an educational charity registered in the United Kingdom,
and are represented in the United States by
ATRIUM PUBLISHERS GROUP
3356 Coffey Lane, Santa Rosa, California 95403.

CONTENTS

Prologue

To the people of the earth

There are no problems on earth.
The earth is beautiful, joyous, cosmic, eternal.
The world is the unhappy superstructure man has imposed on the earth.
The world consists of his problems.

Both earth and world are within you. What you see outside and how it affects you is purely the reflection of what is within you. If you see and feel beauty in your life, it is the earth, the life within you, that you're perceiving. If you see problems and feel unhappy in your life you are looking at the world.

To reach the immortality of life on earth within you, you have to dissolve your attachment to the world. That attachment is devilishly subtle. Any mental or emotional pain you feel at any time is it.

You must see this, and not try to water it down by making exceptions and excuses as the world in you will do. You must face the pain in you, the world in you, without running away into justifications. There are no justifications for unhappiness, none whatever.

To remove any room in you for doubt and interpretations I will repeat the fundamental truth: Any mental or emotional pain you feel at any time in your life, irrespective of the cause, is due to the world in you. You have left the earth and are concentrating on the world.

1

You must see through yourself by recognising that your pain or confusion is your love of the world. You must see through the world by recognising it for what it is, what it has done to you and what it is doing to you. The world is only ever as pressing a problem as your love of it.

By stillness and with courage you must descend to the bottom of the world in you. And then through the bottom of the world in you. That is hell, for a while. But it is your hell, no one else's; the hell you have been pleased to make for yourself on earth by believing in the world and attaching yourself to its values, its ways and the things and persons in it, all of which are always going to leave you or elude you, anyway. Anything you love in the world will cause you pain. That pain is the hell you must pass through – either now, or in the process of your physical death.

Go through hell wrongly and you go round in circles making more problems, more world without end, more hell for yourself. Go through hell rightly and you reunite with the changeless beauty and joy of the earth in yourself as yourself. And in spite of your worldly dreads and fears, you lose nothing. For only fear dies.

Be still and know that I am hell.
Do not complain.
Be valiant.
Be still and know that I am just.
Be patient.

Be still and know that I am God.
For I am God, the spirit of the earth
beneath the world in you.
When you know me in your stillness
you are one with the joy of life on earth
and one with me.

Be still. Listen.
Take no thought.
Descend into yourself.
Come back to earth,
Come back to life.
Descend into me.

The Being Behind the Mask

A LONG, LONG TIME AGO, when human beings were not so fixed in their physical bodies as they are today, there lived a man (or was it a woman?) who made for himself a marvellous mask — a mask that could pull many faces.

The man used to put on the mask and entertain himself by suddenly accosting people and watching their reactions. Sometimes the mask would be laughing, sometimes crying, sometimes grimacing and scowling. His victims were always shocked at the sight of such an extraordinary, unnatural, unfamiliar face — even when it was smiling. But whether they laughed or cried made no difference to him. All he wanted was the excitement of their reactions. He knew he was himself behind the mask. He knew he was the joker — and that the joke was on them.

At first, he'd pop out with the mask on a couple of times a day. Then, as he got used to the excitement and wanted more, he began leaving the mask on all day. Finally, he saw no need to take it off at all — and slept in it.

For years the man wandered through the land enjoying himself behind the mask. Then one day he awoke, feeling a feeling he'd never felt before — he felt lonely, cut-off, something missing.

Jumping up in alarm he stepped out in front of a beautiful woman — and immediately he fell in love with her. But the woman screamed and ran away, shocked by the frightening, unfamiliar face.

'Stop', he cried, 'It's not me!' wrenching at the mask to tear it off.

But it *was* him. The mask wouldn't come off. It was stuck to his

5

flesh. It had become his face.

This man, through his fabulous mask, was the first person to enter this unhappy world.

Time went by. No matter how hard he tried to tell everyone what a disaster he'd brought on himself, no one would believe him. No one was interested in listening anyway, because they'd all copied him. They'd all put on masks of their own — to get the new excitement of playing at being what they were not. Like him, they'd all become the mask.

But now something worse had happened. They'd not only forgotten the joke and the joker; they'd forgotten how to live joyously, as the being behind the mask.

How the man eventually put a stop to the masquerade and returned to his joyous being, is the finale of the story; for all fables must have a happy ending. However, only when you, the reader, are joyous and free of unhappiness now (which is any moment) will the story truly come to an end. For you are the man or woman in the mask.

The mask you are wearing is your personality. Look in the bathroom mirror — that's it. Watch the faces you pull. Sometimes approving; often disapproving. You can't really believe it's you. So you look in every passing mirror, even shop windows, to reassure yourself and confirm it's you.

Sometimes, you even get the weird, irrational feeling of wanting to strip off the mask, don't you? This is not uncommon. It's just that people don't like to talk about it; it sounds silly. But it's not so silly, is it? — when you start being honest.

The biggest load you're carrying in your life is your personality — the strain of pretence. Keeping it up weighs you down and sucks the life out of you.

You blame so many things for the feeling of heaviness and lack of life. You blame your work, your relationships, your diet, your problems. And yet it's your personality that has cut you off from your natural joy and vibrancy.

The personality makes you worried and emotional. It's the cause of your moods and self-doubt, your depressions and times of misery. It confuses your mind. It's fearful of the future and guilty or regretful of the past. It gets listless, bored and restless with the present. It's the unsuspected shadow that slides in between you and your partner. It's the cunning and knowing in the eyes. It lives off every kind of stimulus, good and bad, depression and excitement.

And it's utterly terrified of being found out — discovered as the phoney and spoiler it is.

The personality is the face of dishonesty.

Do you recognise any of these symptoms in yourself?

Then you're ready to begin dismantling the personality. I say dismantle because the personality is a 'mantle', a cloak. And you've thrown the mantle of the personality around you, to shield you from the nastiness of the world and the hurtfulness of people.

You've made the personality your protector. You've handed over much of your authority. So the personality jumps to your defence immediately you feel hurt, threatened or criticised. It hits out for you with piercing or bludgeoning words. Sometimes you wince at its violence and insensitivity. But then it's your champion, your defender. So you meekly go along with its often appalling behaviour, and make excuses for it to yourself. The wily protector, given absolute power, becomes the absolute dictator. And you despair of ever being free.

The truth is, you have no need of this protection. The personality is like a bully at school whose gang you once joined to be on the safe side. After you've grown up he comes back and convinces you that you still need him. He's able to do this because, without knowing it, you harbour all the pain of yesterday — the old fears and hurts of your childhood, your youth and adult life. The bully, knowing your fear, won't leave you alone. And you're terrified to lose his protection.

Notwithstanding this, the personality does have its place and role. It makes a rotten master, but it is a good servant. The servant must no longer be allowed to run your life. It's fouled it up long enough.

Everything you perceive as wrong with the world is the result of someone's personality. In fact, the world itself was constructed by the ignorance of personality. That's why the world is such a cruel, exploitative and dishonest place, compared with the beauty and integrity of the earth and nature. Just as the personality lives off you, and drains your resources, so the world is exhausting the earth's resources.

The world is the personality of the earth.

I'm going to show you your true nature, the nature you were born with, and your false nature, the ground of your personality, the source of your unhappiness. You'll see in a new light how the genius of nature functions; how you came to be separated from that natural genius and how you can return to living in harmony with it. I will explain how the personality develops, where it actually comes from, so that you understand what it is.

What you will gradually realise about the personality is that 'it's not me'. I will describe what is 'me', the real me, the being behind the mask and mantle of the personality. You'll be descending into your own subconscious where the truth of the matter lies. You'll discover a greater presence of authority in yourself. You will take more responsibility for your life, straightening out your messy relationships for good and putting right the situations your personality has left you with.

*

You weren't born with your personality. You were born with nothing. And you can see that by looking at a new baby. A baby is a body of love. It has just come out of the mystery, the almost timeless place that is the womb. There's the beautiful little body, it's lovable movements and sweet, fresh appearance. People love to smell babies. They pick them up and bury their noses in them, and the fragrance is certainly not only talcum powder. There's a smell to a baby that's not of the five senses. It's the psychic smell of innocence. And that innocence is still in you.

Nonetheless, there's something missing in a baby. For all its beauty and wonder it can't cope with the world. Someone has to think for it and protect it. The baby is lacking in the experience of living. We call the acquisition of experience growing up or getting older. That's what you have done. The original baby body of love is still your body but something has happened to it. It has experienced living.

Having gained the experience of all your years, can you say that you are still unburdened like a newborn babe? Are you innocent? Can you say that you are this innocence now, as you were originally? If not, why not?

I'm asking this question of you, the reader, the being who was once a baby and is now an adult. This is about you. I'm speaking about your experience and what is true in your experience is the truth. So what is the truth in your experience?

There are two ways of answering. From the inside or the outside. From the outside, looking in at your tensions, worries and problems, you could say, 'No. I'm burdened by many things that I know and remember, my guilt, my doubts, my fears. I'm free sometimes but I know, as soon as I'm reminded, that I'm not innocent and I start to be anxious and to worry.' But in your deepest and stillest moments you could say, 'Yes. I am innocent.' And that is the truth. For inside you are always the sweet and innocent child you were, no matter how old you are in years. Sweetness and innocence are your nature.

But sweetness and innocence, like a baby, have no place in this world without protection. They will be stamped on, manipulated, exploited, abused and ill-treated. How can I be sweet and innocent like a baby in a world like this? Of course, you can't. Out here, you can't be what you are inside. That's how it seems. But nature, Mother Nature, provides the solution, naturally. The solution is experience.

Living means gathering experience. You can't live without learning the hard way; that if there's glass on the footpath you'd better not tread on it with bare feet. In the same way our beautiful inner nature is protected by the good sense of our experience. But we seem to have forgotten this. When it comes to our emotional lives we ignore our hard-won experience. We repeatedly reach out and embrace what hurts and lacerates us. We put up with and stay with manipulative, emotional, and angry people — hurtful people. We succumb to the selfish demands of their personalities and our own. We allow other people's personalities to live off us, as we live off them. In a mad and perverse trade-off, we agree to exploit each other; and we each suffer in turn.

Do you really want to live with an angry, emotionally demanding or indifferent partner? Of course not. Your innocence can't relate to such destructive love (if you can call that 'love'). But you no longer live from your innocence and pure experience, the love you were born with and the good sense you developed. Your personality has got in-between. And now in your emotional life, your love-life, you're not sure which is which — which is the good sense and which is the spoiler.

Do you want to suffer?

What a silly question. But how else do you explain the way you put up with the unnecessary pain inflicted on you by family and friends? How do you explain the way you expect your loved ones and friends to put up with your unhappy moods?

This odd way of living together you excuse by saying 'No one's perfect. We have to put up with each other's moods and unhappiness'. But I'm asking: Do you? Do you have to put up with the depressions, anger and unhappiness of others? Where did you get that crazy notion?

I'll tell you. It comes from your personality, and the personalities of others. And it's an utter lie. You've been deceived and you don't know it. You don't realise that to the personality, misery, depression and conflict are as satisfying and fulfilling as excitement, adventure and new experience. Personality gets a kick out of both — the up and the down. But you don't. You naturally enjoy the stimulation of new and varied experience, but your true nature doesn't want to hurt anyone in the process. The personality couldn't care less who's hurt or who suffers, you or anyone else. It just wants the experience, good or bad. You truly want the good for yourself and everyone. That's because in your deepest part, in your innocence, you are good; you are love, living love.

Love is your true nature. Personality is your false nature.

Love is your ground.

Out of that inner ground arises your intelligence, which looks out and sees the external world. You are like a lovely flower — your roots planted firmly in love, and your perception of life shining with beauty and the intention of good; for all who can see, to see. That's the truth. That's what you are . . . Or that's what you were before your personality took over. Now you swing between the two. One day you're loving, contented and sweet; the next day bored, depressed, anxious or moody, and those around you suffer.

So where does the personality come from? It comes from pain, emotional pain. While you were gaining experience you unwittingly gathered pain. You accumulated it bit by bit, as an infant, child, teenager and adult. Every time you felt hurt by others, or failed to get what you wanted, a pained emotion arose and stuck to the one before it. Imperceptibly, a ball of past pain grew inside you. And out of that pain arose the personality — the person you are not. You are love. This pained person's name is Fear; an anxious, frightened awareness of the world, a negativity of perception, the terror of being hurt again; pained in the present, as in the past.

Pain is the ground of personality.

You don't realise the pain is there; or that the pain is as intelligent as you are. You don't realise it is speaking and acting through you much of the time, looking for security, to be liked, loved, accepted. It sees the present through the past. It projects its pain on to present events, rendering them painful when they are not. It automatically spoils the good.

Here's an example. When you're making love the fearing personality, looking for comfort to assuage its pain, will often rise up to join in the pleasure. Instantly, a shadow in the form of a reservation, stiffness or wrong word, comes into the good. And the feeling of good vanishes, or is ruined. Have you experienced this? The same thing happens just enjoying someone's company. Have you ever been having a pleasant conversation and one wrong word suddenly spoils or puts an end to the harmony of the situation? That's the personality, butting in.

Have you been suddenly hurt by what someone says? Didn't it spoil your contentment in the present, by making you relate immediately to the pain of some criticism or abuse in the past? Do you see how you put the past on the present?

*

Nature has it's own perfect way of eliminating the pain that gives rise to the personality. And this explains why there's no personality in nature, and no problems.

The first pain in existence is the pain of being born. There you were, like all the other baby mammals, snug in your mother's womb, immersed in a constant fluid warmth of love that supplied everything effortlessly; no need to breathe, to eat, to keep warm, to cry for what you wanted. Then suddenly you were ejected into a world of separation, a strange new place where there was pain and contraction of cold, distance, interruption, hunger, and the relentless need to breathe and communicate by sound. An enormous, traumatising shock.

But in the face of this apparent disaster, Mother Nature as usual took over. Just as she had looked after you inside the womb, she now provided for you from inside your own psyche. Into the shocked vacuum created by being born, nature released a shot of unconditioned psychic plasma. This energetic substance you now call emotion, but at that stage it was the substance of unconditioned love, timeless love. Its function was to temporarily cushion the organism against the shocking interruption of its accustomed flow of time. For in the first moments of shock, as you know from your adult experience, time literally ceases. At birth, without this bridging inflow of love, it would mean death. But love fills the gap by providing an emergency sense of comfort, warmth or continuity. This enables you to go on; although after the acute shock of loss the first impulse is to feel you can't continue.

Nature's psychic response to the pain of birth, as just described, happens in every animal body, not just the human body. Inside every creature body, somewhere in the abdomen, burns a psycho-spiritual flame. The flame is constant and cosmically cold; like the sun's rays, which are cold until they pass through matter. The flame's function is to consume the emergency psychic plasma.

This life-saving cushion of love or consciousness is future time; the future that the organism is moving towards by living and evolving. So the organism has literally borrowed time and security from its own future.

The flame has to consume the plasma as quickly as possible. Speed is vital because 'future time' clearly has no place in the present. In the present, or presence of the body, it immediately degrades into emotion, a negativity. It becomes past time or the past. All emotion is the past reasserting itself; and unless the emotion is consumed swiftly, the organism will start living in the past and be a freak of nature.

Nature's psychic response to shock continues throughout the life of the body. For example, after the shock of a fight or injury, animals tend to seek a quiet place to lie down and lick their wounds. This is to allow the essential flame in the belly to consume, digest and convert the emotion, the past, back into the present or presence of love or consciousness.

The reconverted consciousness then serves another vital purpose which you'll recognise from your own life. It carries the impression of the experience the animal has just been through. The animal has gained or grown in experience and from now on it will instinctively draw upon that experience to protect its survival more efficiently in the future, just as you do after any narrow escape. And so arises the old saying 'An old dog for a hard road'; meaning 'An old experienced dog is better fitted to handle the future'. So the borrowed 'future time' serves a purpose in the present.

Such is the miracle of the divine intelligence that is devising this existence. But the human animal mucks it up, disrupts the divine harmony. The human animal alone holds on to the pain of the event. The human animal thinks about the pain, goes back into the past. The consciousness of the present is absent. This prevents the borrowed time from being converted back into love in the present. For consciousness is the key to harmony and freedom.

The result is, that while gaining experience, the human animal accumulates and regenerates emotional pain, which the animal does not. Both gain the life-saving experience, but only the human suffers emotionally from it.

Why? Why do we do this?

Whatever happened to us?

It's not just what happened to us. It's what's happening now, and happening to our children. We've all been taught to hold on to our pain. And we are teaching our children to do the same. You were first taught this unnatural practice by your mother and father, who were taught by their mother and father, and theirs before them. Then you were taught by the rest of your family and friends and by the society you live in. Today, it is the civilised way of life to hold on to past pain and project the discomfort of it into the world through the personality. Civilised? At any time at least twenty wars are raging on the planet; half the population is starving; much of the other half are exploited by the rest; and the whole population in their private homes or hovels are tyrannising each other with quarrels, arguments, dishonesty and emotional blackmail. And all of it due to people projecting their inner pain through their personalities on to their fellow men and women.

Like the animals, your gaining of experience was natural. But your gathering of pain was not. You were taught that to live you have to suffer, that everybody has to be unhappy sometimes. It's a lie, but you believed it. You believed it because everyone was unhappy and you took their example as the truth.

Who was there to tell you otherwise? Even the priests of Jesus were proclaiming you a sinner, a sufferer. There was nobody to tell anyone the truth because there was nobody to hear. Everybody was listening through the pain of personality. And so it was easy to believe that life is a pain. But it isn't life that is the pain, it's the personality projecting itself on to life.

Nobody is being honest.

All are living a lie. Some say life is good, and the next day they weep with depression or frustration. Others lash their partners and family with hard words and cruel actions, and then protest they love them. Some think they are loving, and spend much of their time complaining and blaming others. Others pollute their homes with foul dark moods and expect to be loved and admired. And many put on cosmetics and a big smile for the public, to cover up their dishonesty to love and life.

Animals do not suffer. Suffering is thinking back; emotionalising over past hurts. Natural creatures don't hold on to their pain. They are instinctive. They feel physical pain just as we do, but when it's over, they instinctively let go of it. The difference between them and you is that you can reflect on the past. You can mentally dwell in the past, in the pain of your emotions. You have self-consciousness, past consciousness; they don't. They depend on pure experience now — no past, no pain in-between.

A dog can be made savage or cowering by ill-treatment. But the animal doesn't dwell on the pain mentally, doesn't think about the past event or the person who caused it. The dog acts from pure experience. If it hears a voice that sounds like the person who caused the pain, it may turn to snarl or cower. But this happens in the moment; and as soon as the moment is passed the dog returns to its natural state.

So animals have no past, no mental awareness of the past. And nor do you, once you detach from the personality. But as you are now, you recall, remember and wallow in the past, in your emotions. You actually re-live the pain when there is absolutely no reason for it. You might be alone in the comfort of your bed, and yet be in the distress of your emotions. You keep pain alive in this way. By holding on to the emotional pain of the past, and indulging in it as a sort of perverse excitement or safe entertainment, you attach yourself to the habit. The attachment to nicotine or heroin is no different. If you continue to indulge in the emotional drug of pain by thinking or talking about it (holding on to it) you'll become addicted. And that's precisely what's happened.

Leave you alone, leave you silent in a chair with your eyes closed for three minutes, and you'll be thinking about the past. In no time your thought will turn to some problem or emotional pain in your life or memory.

Try it now. Put the book down, shut your eyes and be silent for a few minutes. Then come back.

*

'I'm not aware of holding on to any pain. In fact I'm quite free and easy.'

You might say that. The conscious, frontal part of your mind is speaking — speaking for now, the present. But the pain, the ground of the personality, is in the past, in your subconscious; it is underneath what spoke.

I say that emotional pain is stored in the abdomen where there is also a psycho-spiritual flame designed to consume it. But you could say that no doctor has ever found this fundamental pain, or any sign of the flame. The belly or abdomen of course are what you see with your senses, your frontal awareness. I mention it only to mark the spot, as it were. But really the pain that causes your depressions, moods, anger and the like, is in your subconscious. It's hidden completely from sight; but it's not hidden from your experience. When you once heard that a lover had betrayed you, that someone you loved had died or a precious possession was stolen, where did you feel it? You didn't feel it where the doctor could find it. You felt it in your subconscious, in the deep hidden emotional part of you.

There are two places in your subconscious. One is where the psychic ball of pain is lodged and out of which arises your dishonest and fearing personality. The other is where the spiritual flame is. And on top of both lies your frontal awareness, your conscious mind.

Every body loves being in touch with the flame. When they are, they register a feeling or knowledge of joy, easiness, lightness, optimism, sweetness or love. And the conscious mind reflects this through the body as a smiling face, a sprightly step, a harmony or melody in voice and action. Other people are pleased to be with such a body. And the man or woman themselves is contented or fulfilled. But when the frontal mind is connected with the ball of pain, the ground of emotional past, the reaction in mind and body is just the reverse.

There is a difference between personality and character.

Behind every personality, behind every mask, is a character. Most people have heard animal lovers say their pets have distinctive 'personalities'. It makes them uniquely recognisable, they say — endearing, amusing, enjoyable to be with. But that's not the animal's personality; it's the animal's character.

Character is your God-given uniqueness. Character is what you have to return to more consciously in yourself — the character of your joyous being behind the personality.

Everybody without exception has character. The personality so often obscures and deprives you of the pleasure of your character, but this lovable or admirable character appears when the personality is no longer active, when the frontal awareness is connected directly with the flame of innocence. The man or woman is then seen in a different light; the unique character shines forth, and we feel pleased or privileged to be in their company.

Life moves every moment.

The stress of the personality arises out of the terrible contradiction of trying to hold on to existence while the life that you are lets go every moment. Life is ceaseless movement. Everything now is different in some way to what it was yesterday. Why don't we move like life, with the speed or love that lets go every moment?

The answer is in the two words 'life' and 'existence'. Life is in existence but existence is not life. Life is new every moment. Existence also should be new every moment, but we hold on to it and it becomes painful. If you don't hold on to existence, you *are* the life in it, new every moment. Then the two become a harmony. Then being is joyous.

The harmonious interchange between life within and existence without depends on you keeping your psyche free-flowing. The personality clogs the psychic system which is naturally ever-moving. The personality freeze-frames existence. We've freeze-framed our houses, our possessions, our children; and made them 'mine'. We hang

on to them as though they'd disappear if we don't cling to them. It's all
due to the insecure personality that feels it must either hold on or lose
its identity. So we fight people or countries to hold on to what we
have. But life as we see it around us, behind all the personable people
and their personal problems, holds on to nothing.

Life lets go of the last moment every moment.

So now we come to the crucial question. How can you learn to let
go, and be life that is new every moment? How do you start to live
joyously?

And the answer is: You have to get more energy. The remarkable
thing is that all the energy you require is already in you now. But it's
being wasted by your personality. There is only so much energy in
your system, your body. It's not unlimited, but there is sufficient to
enable you to realise the truth; to return you to the joyous life behind
the mask — your original, vast and untroubled state of being.

You are dissipating your energy out into existence through the
personality, instead of using it to stay in your reality. The mask is kept
on by energy going out. As you deny the projection of the personality,
you conserve energy. When enough energy is retained, the mask
collapses. It loses its independent and selfish existence.

I'm going to show you where you're wasting this energy. Since you
will then be conscious of it — because you've seen it in your own
experience — you'll begin to stop the leakage. You'll have more energy
to address other wasteful mannerisms, attitudes and behaviour.
Gradually you'll become more conscious, more responsible, more
authentic. Your character will reveal itself and your personality will be
less in control of your life.

I am going to mention ten things for you to do or stop doing.
They will conserve your energy. To begin with it will be hard. As you
get deeper into the process you may become confused. The
personality will always be trying to bamboozle you and make you give
up. But keep going: the ten exercises will always be here to remind
you and guide you. Your own undeniable experience that it's working
will be the demonstration of the truth. You will notice that you are

lighter, easier, more joyous. A new harmony will start pervading your whole life, within and without.

• *Stop talking about the past.*

The personality lives off the past, feeds off you telling your story. Each time you hear yourself indulging in this, stop.

The more you practise, the easier it gets. You may lose some friends who'll say you're getting dull; you're losing your former interesting and stimulating personality. You'll know by this that you're doing well.

There will be times when you have to refer to the past. To break the old habit, initially you must be extreme. The extremity is not to say *anything* that refers to the past. This includes what happened a minute ago, unless there's a purely practical reason for speaking such as 'Did you post that letter?'

Don't tell your sad, sad, story.

By stopping talking about the past you will eventually stop thinking about the past. And that will be the beginning of the end of worry.

• *Be true to the situation.*

Be true to the situation and not to your personal likes and dislikes. The personality lives off emotional swings between what you like and what you don't like. It uses the dynamic of the pendulum to keep itself going.

You can't be sure of your likes and dislikes. They change with experience and the years. So be true to the situation, to the event or circumstance you're facing.

What does the situation require? It may not be what suits you personally. For example, if you're employed to do a job, be true to what you're paid for, not to whether you like it or don't like it. If you insist on reacting in dislike, be true to the situation and resign, because clearly, you won't be doing a good job.

The personality, remember, will actually enjoy the conflict in situations like that. It wants you to go on doing a job and not liking it because then you can complain and emotionalise about it to your friends. This consumes energy which should be used for taking action one way or the other. Either you do the job by giving up your attitude, or you quit. That's being true to the situation. Action always clears deadlocked energy.

- *Give up your dishonesty.*

Give up being dishonest to yourself and your life. Any time you're angry, resentful or depressed, it means you are not being honest: you are not facing life as it is.

Anger arises because you are not getting your own way. Instead of being angry you should be looking at what practical action you can take to get around the obstruction. If there's no practical action you can take, your desire is impractical at this time. To be honest you must face that fact and give up your wanting.

Remember, the mask of your personality is dishonesty itself. It hides the fact that if you have a very exciting experience today, you're likely to undergo depression in a couple of days. The personality gets it's satisfaction both ways; and you pay for it.

- *Don't talk unless you've got something to say.*

The personality is always talking. Talking consumes enormous energy. So this exercise is to learn to talk less.

Talking is talking *about* something — having a discussion, giving your opinions, speculating, rationalising and repeating what you've heard.

In this exercise you learn the difference between 'talking' and 'speaking'. For instance, everyone talks about what the politicians should do. You can't talk about what the politicians should do unless you do something yourself towards righting the situation; write to the politicians, phone them or cast your vote. Then you'll be taking action and able to *speak* from your own experience. Otherwise you're just a talker. Only action, or speaking what you live, is true.

• *No more complaining and blaming.*

Complaining about your life, and blaming other people and things for your difficulties, is one of the main leakages of energy. When you hear yourself doing this, stop.

The truth is you are responsible for your life. If you're not responsible, it's not your life; and that's absurd. Similarly, if you blame something else for what happens to you, you're giving up responsibility by giving it to others.

To be responsible is to be responsible for everything that happens to you, unfolding as your life. Indeed, there are continual difficulties you have to face. They may seem to have been caused by other agencies. But you have to do your best to sort them out. That's life.

You don't complain when you get a promotion at work, do you? You don't blame the boss. You feel you deserved it; that you must have earned it. In other words, you accept that you were responsible. So how can you duck out from being responsible for all the not-so-good things that happen to you?

Again, it's the personality being two-faced, not being straight. It presents life as it is not. And gets away with it while you continue to blame and complain.

Now to break some seemingly trivial habits that nonetheless eat up vital energy.

• *Don't fidget.*

Don't allow your fingers to fiddle with a pencil or other knick-knack. Don't drum your fingers on the table.

And especially for young men: When seated, don't quiver or tremble your leg. And don't crack your knuckles.

• *Stop indulging your mouth.*

Don't chew gum — unless you chew it intentionally to get the flavour and freshen the mouth. Then spit it out, but not on the pavement please (another thoughtless action of the personality).

Never lick your fingers after touching food. Once you start touching and licking it will become habitual and even your best friends won't tell you.

Don't ask for morsels to taste from your partner's plate. Either go halves or order some for yourself. That's the personality's greed and it's craving for experience, not being responsible for what it wants.

- *Beauty tips for women.*

Don't run your fingers back through your hair when you're talking or making a point. And don't play with it, by curling strands of hair around your finger.

If you wear make-up, start leaving it off. It only takes three months to stop thinking you look like a ghoul. Make-up, of course, is a personality projection, a cover-up, hiding the awful truth of the mask.

- *Tackle habitual small talk.*

Remember that the personality depends on habitual unconsciousness. Stop the conversational habit of using expressions like 'darling', 'honey', 'my love' and 'my dear' when addressing your partner, friends or casual contacts. If anything, use the person's correct name.

After you've broken the habit you'll find the endearing expression occurs naturally and appropriately. But to begin with, to break the habit and make the situation conscious, don't use such terms.

Don't pat your partner down with silky words and actions when you know you're planning to be dishonest, or you've done something they don't like. Instead, say 'I'm moved to pat you down because I don't want you to react to what I've done or what I'm about to do'. Then tell them straight what you've done or what you're about to do. Mostly you'll find that you won't do what you were going to do; or you'll just do it and cop the force of their disapproval. At least you'll be honest; and such honesty loosens the mask.

Don't say: 'What I mean is . . .' and 'You know?' Or any similar fill-in phrase. These are all unconscious in-words of the western personality, now globally habitual.

And don't say 'To be honest . . . ' because that implies you're about to be dishonest. Or that you're usually a liar.

Such phrases have no real meaning and are actually the mask talking.

• *Don't pull faces.*

For example: don't frown, screw up your face or look at the ceiling before you answer a question. That's the personality pretending to be serious, sincere or intelligent; pretending to be thinking deeply.

Know that the personality is a performer and communicates through grimaces and other facial antics, to assert its existence. The more serene and unaffected your face, the more in touch you are with your being.

Those are the ten exercises. Practise them in your daily life over the next twelve months or so, and you'll slowly separate from the domination of the personality.

✳

If you are a parent you can see in your children how the personality operates and how the mask is put on. You will see how the developing child, at only a few months, actually starts to mimic unhappy mannerisms or hostile and argumentative behaviour.

If your child sees you pulling faces to show dislike or disgust or to drive home an argument, it will copy the facial expressions and physical stances, even without feeling those emotions. By copying and putting on the mask it will learn to actually be angry and feel anger.

Here is an exercise that you can do with young children. I suggest you tell them the fable of 'The Man and the Mask'. Tell them the story as I gave it to you at the beginning of this; and listen seriously to their observations. Answer their questions honestly, and give them all the time they need to make their comments. The exercise is for both you and the children to see how the personality operates, and how it interrupts and spoils the harmony of the body, the home and the life.

A child puts on personality for two basic reasons. First, it wants attention; and second, a sympathetic reaction to whatever face it pulls — just like in the fable. A child will pretend to be coy or shy by using mannerisms and facial expressions it has seen somewhere, in the family, at school or on television. At first the child doesn't feel the emotion behind the act. But when encouraged by adults, it enjoys their reactions and starts to believe and become its own performance — just like the joker who forgot himself.

Remember, the personality lives off every kind of emotion. It is just as fulfilled by the negative vibration of anger and frustration, as it is by excitement and getting its own way.

Now, here's an intelligence test.

Please ask yourself this question: Do I want to be with, live with or love somebody who's ever moody, angry, restless, sullen, resentful or depressed?

If the answer is 'no', then the next question is: Why do I believe that anyone would want to live with me while I have those emotions?

*

As you dismantle the personality and become more one with life, you will start to feel some disintegration of yourself. You will feel at times you are 'nothing', and that you're losing your identity. Know that it's your personality you're losing, not your identity. Nothing you are or have will disappear. All that goes is the attachment, the identification with the things the personality calls 'me and mine'. And that includes your most intimate and treasured notions of what life and love is about.

For in the end I realise that nothing is 'mine', not even my own body. I am behind it all — the being behind the mask in the bathroom mirror.

I am the end of the masquerade.

Now back to the fable, and the happy ending. It took many, many years but in the end the man in the mask tired of his miserable up-and-down existence.

One day he rested beside a lake in the forest and gazed into the transparent stillness of the water. It reminded him of something, deep within.

'I'm enjoying this', he reflected, 'But is that the joy? Or am I the joy?'

'I'm the joy!' he cried, jumping to his feet, 'I'm the joy of life behind all I see.'

He gave thanks. And he never looked for excitement again. For he'd found the secret of living joyously.

The secret is joy.

The man looked up and saw the beauty around him. And then realised the truth that set him free.

I'm not this or that. I'm nothing seen or heard. I'm joy. I'm the joy of life behind it all. The whole world is my wonderful mask and I am content behind it.

*

Life is to be enjoyed, to be made conscious by enjoying it. For joy is consciousness. When you enjoy anything you do, you are conscious. If you enjoy dancing, you're conscious while dancing. If you enjoy gardening, you're conscious while gardening. If you enjoy your work, you're conscious while working. Enjoy every moment of your life and you're living joyously. It's as simple as that.

Joy or consciousness is your natural state. It's always there. It's like the sun that is always shining above the shadow of the earth. Stop living in your own shadow and the sun, the joy, immediately shines.

Nothing positive can be done to find joy. It's the practice of negation, shedding the shadow, that does it.

Living joyously is the joy of clarity — no problems. My whole life is then a joy or clarity of being — a being of joy and clarity.

This is there now inside you, just waiting to be lived. You don't have to strive for it, search for it or make it. It's you. It's yours, your very being.

The Truth of Life on Earth

I AM GOING TO TELL YOU the truth of life on earth. But you are not going to like it.

You are not going to like it because you already know this truth and have chosen to forget it. You are determined not to be reminded. So you are going to make excuses for not hearing it, for avoiding it and for continuing to forget it.

Here it is:

You have no right to be unhappy — ever.

But you think you have. So in your ignorance you live intimately and willingly with unhappiness; you have made a partner of it in your life. At any moment you are likely to be depressed, sullen, worried, resentful, frustrated, fretful, moody. No one can rely on you to be without unhappiness for long. It is closer and dearer to you than any man, woman or child in your life. So it regularly comes between you and others, plunging even your cherished relationships into discord and argument. Undeterred, however, you persist in living through your spiky, troublesome emotions, forcing those around you to live through them too, until it suits you to be agreeable and nice again . . . till the next time.

The horror is, you believe that living this way is natural to life on earth. So you tolerate and excuse your sordid, unhappy moods. And by your example you infect the children with this terrible, unnatural disease. While throughout, you think you are lovable or that you deserve to be loved more. You are irresponsible. You dishonour life on earth. Because you love your unhappiness, and not life.

Are you doubting this? Then let us test your integrity.

Next time you are moody, irritable, worried, sulkily silent, impatient or depressed, will you give it up immediately, now, and come to life? Or will you hold on grimly to this ugliness, your unhappiness? Will you defend it? Buckle down with true grit to your right to be unhappy? Fight for it? As perhaps you are inclined to do now? Anything you cling to with such devotion and loyalty you obviously love.

You have conveniently chosen to forget that your unhappiness is yours alone. You alone are responsible for it as your personal contribution to unhappiness on earth. It can be there in you only for as long as you are sufficiently selfish, immature and insensitive to put up with it. No one else can be rid of it for you. No one else wants your unhappiness, only you.

So why are you dishonest with yourself?

Why, when you are unhappy, do you pretend to complain that you don't want to be unhappy? When it is you all the time doing it, holding on to it?

Now let me remind you of the rest of the truth of life on earth.

You have no right to be unhappy, ever — because life is good.

And life is always good now. Let someone press a pillow over your face, now, or when you are unhappy, and you will get the point. Be told that you have cancer and a month to live, and watch every problem, every pathetic bit of unhappiness in your life now, vanish miraculously. Instantly you will discover that life is good. And that it is good now, this moment and every moment.

You will realise that life is not in yesterday or tomorrow, not in that past and future dreamland of unhappiness where you breed and hatch your moodiness and resentments. Whatever day you die — and it is always closer than you think — your one wish will be that you had realised the truth of life.

Must you be forced to face death to know that life is good?

There is no unhappiness in events.

Any unhappiness is in you — in your holding on to the right to be unhappy because things have changed, as they must. No one can escape the events of life. But in the blindness of being unhappy you fail to see that shocking events only exist to shock you into waking up and realising the truth of life. That is the purpose of living, which you have also chosen to forget.

You always have a good excuse to justify your unhappiness. Always someone or something is to blame; but never you, who is the only one to blame. You smoulder angrily because of what someone has done to you. You are bitter or moping because someone has failed you, betrayed you, let you down. Or you are inconsolable, lost in grief, because a lover, a loved one, your job or your money has died or left you.

That is living like most people do. But it is not life. Living that way and ignoring the truth of life has to be traumatic or painful because everything you live for must die, change or pass away — while you keep hoping it won't. Trying to live with such hopelessness, such pointlessness, is unhappiness.

You are not just living. You are life.

You are life itself, personified on earth. And you are life all the time, behind the incessant ups and downs of the personality — not just some of the time. Life does not change or pass away. Life goes on. Has there ever been a moment when you did not go on, when you did not get through even the direst crisis? Of course not.

Life is good because life is true. And it is every moment — once you surrender the right to be unhappy.

Surrender it now and you are free.

You may not be unhappy at this moment. But you will be tomorrow or the next day. Happy today, unhappy tomorrow — that's normal. And that is unhappiness.

29

You cannot be happy: to think that or want it is ignorance because whatever you aim for or achieve cannot last; and then you will be unhappy again. You can only be free of unhappiness. That alone lasts.

When you are free of unhappiness, what is there to want?

Unhappiness is ignorance.

Ignorance is the accumulation of all the past emotional hurt and pain you are pleased to ignore in yourself because you feel it is too painful to face. Why face it when you can run from it? The trouble is that when you run from ignorance or emotional pain in yourself you run from life; and sooner or later you start to feel dead, don't you?

Unhappiness is substantial.

Unhappiness lives in you. At this moment, even though you may be tranquil or untroubled, unhappiness is there. Periodically and inevitably it will rise up and you will be unhappy without knowing why. You will be depressed, self-doubting, self-pitying, lonely, resentful or sad.

Unhappiness is not natural in you. It has invaded you from the external world since your conception in the womb. The invasion started through the medium of similarly acquired unhappiness residing in your mother's body. And since infancy, due to your parents' ignorance of the cause of unhappiness, and the ignorance of your associates, teachers and yourself, unhappiness has been allowed to continue to enter and grow in you. It is now a sturdy, health-eroding, degenerative, living body, the same age as yourself. This is your 'unhappy body'.

The substance of your 'unhappy body' is your emotions. You may think you get pleasure out of your emotions. But it's a fickle pleasure, an emotional high that never lasts because its opposite pole is a fickle pain, an emotional low. The two are a see-saw. You can't have one without the other.

Emotional pleasure arises from the stimulus of excitement. Then, as the excitement dies, the pleasure disappears. And you gradually become bored, restless, confused or unhappy — until another stimulus comes along. You are up for a while, then down. That is your life. Up-and-down. Pleasure precedes pain: pain precedes pleasure. And in-between the dreaded emptiness of boredom and aloneness prevents you from making the connection or seeing the truth of how your life is being manipulated.

Aloneness, like boredom, is intolerable to the emotions. It is felt as acute loneliness, or isolation. To the emotions, aloneness and boredom are like death, the end of any hope of stimulus or excitement. So, to avoid this dreaded state, if there is no exciting or pleasurable activity to look forward to, the emotions revive in you the stimulus of past unhappy feelings. You are then depressed or 'down' without knowing why.

In time, as your 'unhappy body' develops, you begin to enjoy subconsciously the see-sawing stimulus, the downs as well as the ups. Whether the emotions are pleasurable or painful is no longer very important. As long as they are stimulated or active — on a high or a low you feel emotionally alive; and this is preferable by far to the feeling of being emotionally dead or alone.

By the time your 'unhappy body' matures, you are emotionally hooked — addicted to the perverse pleasure of emotional pain or unhappiness. You cling to it as your moods and depressions. You enjoy it.

When you're next moody or depressed, will you give it up, now?

No. You'll say you can't or you won't. You enjoy your unhappiness too much to let go of it. The fact that it's painful — that at the time you protest how unhappy you are — is irrelevant. The truth is you prefer this pain you know to the simple pain you refuse to face, the pain of being alone without stimulus.

And why won't you face it?

Because of fear. Facing it is like dying. But it's only the fear dying. Only fear dies. And if you confront the pain, if you face it for long enough, you break through into the blue sky of freedom and joy.

*

Since the substance of your 'unhappy body' is composed entirely of this painful emotional material, I will refer to it from now on as your *emotional body*.

Your emotional body does not have everything its own way. It is continuously being undermined by your natural untroubled being. In fact, in the loving and spiritual moments of your life, the emotional body is actually being reduced. But because in the rest of your life the cause of unhappiness is being avoided, the emotional body is continually being replenished; and you are forced to continue sharing your life with your unhappy moods and depressions. When you, your natural being, are buoyant, the emotional body is dormant. When the emotional body is buoyant, you are dormant. Each of you has your days in the one physical body.

It is a very strange way of life. As everyone is living it, or doing it, it is said to be normal, which is true. But it is not natural.

What is normal is not natural.

The natural state of man and woman is joy within. Beneath your normal to-and-fro emotions, you are joy. And unlike anything that is normal, natural joy, or bliss within, has no opposite.

*

All the unhappy moments of your life live on in you now in your emotional body. Every single hurt of childhood is still there — the times you sobbed in your locked room, lost your closest friend, were bullied at school, pined and fretted out of loneliness and injustice. All those unhappy, unconsoled children or emotions weep on in you, the adult of the little boy or little girl you were.

Those earliest of emotions did not remain fragmented. In their pain and isolation they drew together inside you. Building up one on top of the other in living layers of feeling, they compressed themselves into a sad and lonely emotional 'ball', centred in your stomach area.

In early childhood this small, moody, unhappy ball had little strength or force. You were easily distracted from it and able to throw off your gloomy self pretty quickly. But this changed with puberty.

Puberty marks the arrival of pure sexual energy. This acts on the natural body in a pure way; but in the emotional body it plays quite a different part.

In the naturally happy physical body the inflowing sexual or reproductive energy brings pure sensual wisdom or power; and throughout puberty, under its deep, enriching influence, the body matures beautifully and naturally. Moreover, the new energy gradually imparts to it the natural or divine ability to create more natural happiness or joy in other bodies — the natural happy bodies it is capable of making love with perfectly and instinctively; and the happy baby bodies that would naturally be formed and born out of their unions.

This was the supremely beautiful and yet thoroughly practical design for life or love on earth. And it still is, if you want it. Combined with the self-consciousness that of all the species only man and woman possess, the result was to be a continuous expansion in the flesh of the joy and wonder of consciously participating in life on this planet. But the presence of the emotional body ruined it, for you and for everyone.

Unhappiness is completely parasitic and destructive of the good and the right — the natural. In nature, no unhappiness or emotion exists in its own right; no provision is made for its survival or evolution in any organ or organism, including the human body. Consequently, the unnatural existence of the emotional body inside the physical natural body at the climacteric of puberty created an enormous distortion and distraction in the natural perception of the senses.

The full extent of this distortion and distraction is before you now as your pain-and-pleasure existence, the world of problems and ill-health, which everyone correctly regards as normal, and erroneously regards as natural and unavoidable.

The new incoming sexual energy, while greatly strengthening the happy physical body, also necessarily strengthens the parasitic emotional body. While the physical is able to adapt perfectly to the transforming potency of the energy and able to reach the full power of sexual maturity and sexual wisdom, the young emotional body is utterly incapable of accommodating it or coping with it. As wisdom or maturity emerge only from inner joy, the emotional body cannot receive the generative power of the energy. It can only react as a resistance. In pushing its way through this resistance, the purity and power of the sexual energy degenerates into the impurity of force.

Force is neither power nor strength.

Force is the beginning of violence. And all violence begins in the unhappy and insecure emotional bodies of men and women.

An early appearance of this force in the world is the normal headstrong ignorance and wilful independence of adolescence. This expresses itself as a more or less blind determination to find pleasure or love in excitement, not in oneself.

Adolescent (and subsequent adult) behaviour is also determined by another remarkable effect of the incoming sexual power. The pure energy of puberty immediately begins destroying the unhappy emotional body by purging the force. This expulsion of force manifests externally in adolescence as an almost constant psychic or nervous discontent — a wanting to be always mentally, emotionally or physically engaged in some activity; not necessarily doing anything but wanting to do it.

This same restlessness, mellowed by the weight of experience, continues in you, the adult today, making it virtually impossible for you to remain free of thought or at peace with yourself for any length of time without the aid of some external stimulus.

The sexual part of unhappiness is the desire for instant pleasure.

After puberty, the hold of the emotions is much tighter than in early childhood. As an adolescent you could no longer be distracted from your emotions. Unsuspectingly you were attaching to them by amusing and gratifying yourself with the new and stimulating pleasure of sexual or romantic fantasising.

By indulging in any kind of erotic imagining you were playing with the full force of unhappiness. But of course in your ignorance you did not know it, any more than you do today if you continue to indulge in it. All that mattered to the adolescent emotional body was that the incoming sexual energy offered the ultimate in excitement — a fantastic new means of selfish pleasure. The fact that there were strings attached (that there is no such thing as a free lunch) never occurred to you.

Underneath all the imaginings and turbulent emotions provoked by the images, the inflowing stream of pure sex energy is absolutely constant and unvarying in its richness and fullness. But felt through the resistance of the emotional body the energy appears to be intermittent. It rises as an exciting sexual urge, which produces an intense emotional high until the sexual stimulus ends, the energy slows down and you feel calm or normal again. The emotional body is never stable; it is either going up or going down. Much of this occurs beneath your awareness. After being excited and then seeming to calm down, the emotional body keeps on slowing down beneath your awareness until sooner or later, within hours or days, its vibration reaches the dreaded in-between point felt as boredom, isolation or aloneness. To get out of this, and in an attempt to regain the lost pleasure or stimulus of the high, the emotional body forces you to think about past exciting experiences — usually sexual. This makes it vibrate at the intensity of a high again and the feeling is very pleasant. (How often have you done this lying in bed or in a hot bath?) Again, as soon as the imaginative stimulus ends, when you stop thinking or turn your attention elsewhere, the emotional body continues to vibrate on its own. Since it is an unhappy organism it cannot help but create in itself an unhappy effect — the opposite of the high, an equally intense depression. This surfaces in your awareness hours or days afterwards as a nasty, gloomy feeling of lack; you are depressed or moody without knowing why. This soon turns into a desire or craving to repeat the missing pleasure, which drives you to engage in activity, again trying to repeat the pleasure of the high. The activity is usually sexual, or a normal self-gratifying substitute such as appeasing the appetite for food, spending, alcohol, clothes, entertaining, money — some sort of passing pleasure. Inevitably, this leads to more discontent and unhappiness; and in turn to more craving, more misguided action, more pain and so on.

This cycle of pleasure and pain continues uninterrupted for the entire life; or until a conscious stand is made to dissolve the emotional body and be what you are.

*

New pains arrive thick and fast as a result of fresh sexual experiences and pressures, adding to the residual ball of unhappiness. You learn to fear what caused them, and how to erect emotional barriers to prevent the same pains hurting you again. These self-protective devices grow into emotional calluses which insulate and dull your feelings. Gradually you feel more and more dead. The enjoyment and delight of life without the aid of some stimulus or excitement becomes almost impossible. You wonder what happened to the delicious alive feeling of your youth. It hasn't gone: you've just covered it over with hardened emotion — fear.

Do you recognise this in yourself?

In love, you become especially self-guarding. You give just so much of yourself but never all — because you are afraid, though not quite sure what you're afraid of; you're just afraid, cautious, holding back. And when you do give yourself as much as you are able, you get hurt again. Because you choose your partners through the emotions of your emotional body, inevitably your choices bring unhappiness.

The emotional body is devoid of love and in relationships it looks to get the love and happiness it does not have. Since you can't receive what you can't give, the partnership of emotional bodies invariably ends in emotional strife and torment, with both people crying out in pain, demanding love. Or the alliance ends in compromise, either wishy-washy or painful — a callous denial of love and life, cosily called comfort, convenience, compatibility or companionship.

Sooner or later your love-life is disastrous. Your tender dreams of love and romance are consistently punctured, bruised and violated. Each hurt, which in your ignorance you thought was over, that you'd got over, every disappointment and heartbreak joins your residual emotional body. And they weep and grieve again as the moods and depression you can't explain, yet cling to as yourself.

*

This book was written for you, the man or woman reading it now, to expose your unhappiness and show you how you can start to dissolve your own emotional body. The book is for you. It has no value unless you are willing to start ridding yourself of unhappiness now.

So far you have been reading about the personality and the way unhappiness grows in you. Now you actually have to face the truth of life, by learning how to handle living, for you cannot escape the events of life. Then you have to start the long and sometimes painful process of getting rid of the unhappiness that has accumulated in you.

It is up to you to do it, and so make the blessed earth that much happier where you are.

*

To rid yourself of unhappiness you must first prevent any more unhappiness gathering in you.

Unhappiness always begins now.

Unhappiness is substantial and it gathers now. Any unhappiness you remember and grieve over is already past and resident in you, so that is not the unhappiness that begins now. Unhappiness begins with events which are immediately identifiable, events like crashing your car, being parted from someone you love, a sexual disaster, a death, losing your job — any sort of shock. The task is to prevent the emotion of the moment from entering you. This requires immediate action, that instant.

First action: face the fact that the event has actually happened.

The initial reaction normally is one of disbelief. This is an attempt by the emotional body to escape or look away from reality in order to avoid shock. It allows time for emotion to rush in; and you lose your presence.

First perceive the fact.

You do this by not seeing the event as a problem; that is, by not thinking what it will mean to you in the future, or how it is going to affect you. You must stay in the present. You must be real. And to be real means to be present where you are at the moment.

The future has not come. The fact is: your car or part of your life is changed in front of you. Don't interpret. Don't analyse. You must see the event only as it is, without putting any imagination or conclusions onto it. Then any physical action required of you will immediately occur in your awareness — without you having to worry or think.

It is now alone that matters. The instant you leave the present by thinking about the future or the past you will be unhappy. You will allow emotion in. That also applies after the event. You must not think back on it, must not go over it in your mind.

The shock of the event at the time cannot be avoided. But shock is not emotion. Shock is a vacuum — the vacuum in which self-change can occur. Shock cuts out all thought, all continuity of the past in you. At the moment of shock, you are new, if you can be present. And the possibility of fundamental, radical self-change is enormous. The panic and worry only start when you allow thoughts to re-enter and stir up the old emotional body permitting more emotion, more unhappiness to pour in.

Keep to the action.

You must keep to action, moment to moment, as dictated by the energy of the event itself. See the event, the scene itself, and you will see with clarity what has to be done, if anything.

Don't do what you think. Do what is right. And what is right is reflected in what is — the event as it is in the world now in front of you, not in your imagination. If nothing is to be done, you will see that; so then do nothing. But don't think.

If you allow your mind to move outside the now by projecting into the future or past, even by reflecting on what someone might say or think, you will turn the incident into a problem. It will then no longer be perceived for what it is, a pure happening. You will have injected fear, your emotional unhappiness, into it.

If you can keep it as a pure happening (by not conceiving it to be what it is not) it will not cause you unhappiness, now or in the future. Keep the unhappiness out of now and you keep it out of the future. Other events flowing from the incident will then fall into place rightly, in their own moment.

If you are feeling emotional pain, it means you are not seeing straight. You have short-circuited yourself, cut off from the natural flow. You are thinking, projecting your fears and uncertainties (your emotional body) onto the event. The event will then have to reflect some of the same unhappy emotions back to you in subsequent events, which will appear to contain more of the same problem.

In the next few paragraphs I am going to explain just what this means and the truth behind it. It is one of the great liberating truths of existence. To connect energetically with it in yourself, you may have to read the explanation several times, and at more than one sitting. But when you make the connection it will release great self-knowledge or spiritual clarity. Here it is:

Everything happens in your consciousness.

Everything happens in your consciousness; that is how you are conscious of what happens.

What you imagine to have happened, such as what happened while you were asleep last night, is an entirely different thing. That is the working of the mind, not of consciousness. Consciousness is behind the mind and provides the consciousness that allows the mind to work and reflect. The mind is dependent on the consciousness; but consciousness is not dependent on the mind.

Let me give you another example of the difference between the two in your daily life. If your car is crashed in your absence by another driver, the event did not occur in your consciousness. The event in that case occurs in your consciousness only at the moment you are informed of it. And how you react or respond to it in that moment determines whether you make a problem of it and create for yourself a succession of problems to follow.

In other words, the clarity with which you are able to perceive an event determines how the events and the circumstances flowing from it will affect you in the future. If an event is seen as a problem when it happens, whatever happens afterwards in that connection will be seen as an extension of the same problem, and will in fact become a part of the same problem. Which means the event will be followed by a succession of other problematical events; such as, if you crash your car, the problem of getting the damaged vehicle to the garage, being without the car for several weeks, finding the money to pay the insurance excess and so on.

Mankind has come to accept this normal problematical sequence of living as the unquestionable natural flow of events: every problem requires other problems, or time and effort, to solve it. But this is not the truth. And it is not natural or necessary at all. It is indeed what generally happens, but only because everyone creates problems in their consciousness out of events. Once you cease doing this, once you begin seeing each event as unique in this moment and having no problematical continuity or future, the entire dynamic changes. This is because of the power of your consciousness.

Your consciousness (not your mind) is the most powerful, creative thing in existence. It directs your life from behind the mind, completely faithful to how you perceive life. It does not force anything on you: it creates for you, according to the clarity of your perception. For you are in charge of your life and how you see life is how it affects you, or how it must be. If you perceive problems, your consciousness is compelled to create problems. If, however, you start to resist problem-making and see events only as they happen, then your consciousness is free to begin working naturally, as it is supposed to, without any more problems being created. This is the miracle of life, the miracle of consciousness, that eliminates all unhappiness.

Now let me give you the key to it all. The truth which makes this miracle possible is that every event that happens in your consciousness is the natural answer or solution to a previous event. Any delay or problem is only in the mind.

Don't be the problem: be, and the solution arrives.

40

If you do not give an event a future or an effect in time, by thinking it's going to be a problem or cause a problem, any seeming difficulty will be quickly cancelled out by some other event. All you have to do is be and the solution will arrive.

To illustrate: if you crash your car, a tow-truck comes around the corner or someone offers you a tow; someone out-of-the-blue lends you a car while yours is being repaired; you receive a sum of money you weren't expecting to pay the insurance excess. Whatever the situation, there are no problems: because you are not making them.

All you have to do is respond to events as they occur and keep the emotional problem-making out of your consciousness, by not reacting anxiously or impatiently. What is necessary will be provided by the natural unfolding of events.

The secret is: the less you make a problem of your life, of any event in your life, the less time or emotion is created between the event and its natural solution. In short, you reduce and finally eliminate time as a difficulty or restriction. Events then flow timelessly and the life is sweet, easy and effortless — even though to others it may seem to be a problem.

It all comes down to this: you make the problem, you magnify it, and then you think that in time or by your actions you dissolve or solve it. When all you are doing, with all your worrying and frustration, is delaying the solution which would have come earlier, anyway. There is no problem in the first place.

You — your unhappiness that prevents you from seeing the simple truth of life — are the only problem. You, the problem-maker, merely get in the way as the pain and confusion of it all. Rid yourself of the problem, your unhappiness, and all problems disappear, all unhappiness disappears.

*

To dissolve the emotional body that has built up in you since birth is a big job. It is harder for some than for others, and sometimes it takes only a few words of truth to communicate the whole idea: the man or woman immediately sees what has to be done and starts getting on with it, with a tremendous feeling of relief and discovery.

To start with you have to be able to feel the presence of your emotional body within you. If you cannot feel it, you can't begin to deal with it.

When it is rampant and active, such as when you're angry or depressed, the emotional body is likely to be too powerful for you to separate from it. You will become identified with it, absorbed by it and lose yourself in it. So you must begin to identify it in normal times, like now, when it's probably just dormant, ticking over.

The surface of your emotional body can be felt now by closing your eyes and focusing your inner attention on the feeling, the sensation, in the area of your stomach. This means feeling the actual feeling, the physical sensation, inside your body. Please close your eyes and feel it now.

You may have difficulty discerning the sensation unless you have become sufficiently still through the practice of right meditation. Nevertheless, it will come, if you don't try. (Not all meditation is right. In right meditation the mind is still and the attention is one with the reality you are feeling or being at any moment).

Through that sensation all your moods and depressions rise up from the subconscious. If you have just had an argument, the emotional stress will be felt first in the abdomen, around the navel. But the stress will spread quickly through the whole of your body, especially to the heart, chest, throat and eventually the head where it will create a headache, tiredness, confusion or some other distracting reaction.

Remember, the emotional body is as alive and intelligent as you are. It does not want to be found out and seen as separate from you. So it will try to distract you, and it usually succeeds. One way it does this is by affecting other parts of the body with aches and pains. These are not lasting because the emotional body does not have the staying power to affect any area for more than an hour or so; although it will keep bringing the aches and pains back from time to time. However, its main distraction is to make you think. Thinking will certainly stop you getting at the root of the emotional body, the unhappiness in your belly.

You must understand that due to your neglect and ignorance, the unhappy emotional body has taken charge of much of your inner self, your subconscious. It will not surrender. You have to get in there and root it out, consciously, energetically.

To dissolve the emotional body requires action, now. You must make a start somewhere, and now, this moment, is always where you begin. Pause at the end of this paragraph, close your eyes and be as still and silent as you can within. Feel the feeling, the physical *sensation* in your body around the belly.

What you are feeling *is* it.

It is the residual emotion, the unhappy tenant of your body. It may seem harmless and very ordinary, if you are not disturbed. But once you're upset, it will be an intense feeling, a compulsive urge to worry or do something other than focus on the discomfort of the feeling.

If at this moment you cannot feel the feeling of yourself, it means you are not yet still enough. You are unlikely to make any real progress until you learn to meditate rightly. Again, immediate action is required: arrange to learn right meditation. (Some of my other books will help you).

While focusing on sensation, do not think about what you are doing. Just do it. Thinking means projecting into the future or back into the past — distraction. The emotional body itself makes you think because it knows that while you are thinking you are dissipating the only energy that can destroy it. In other words it is distracting your conscious attention.

Look, energetically.

You do this by holding the sensation with your attention. Perceive it, feel what is there. Don't draw conclusions. Conclusions are thinking, not looking.

By looking energetically like this with the attention, you are seeing and discovering what is, without putting a name to it. The beautiful simplicity and effectiveness of this process is a most difficult thing for people to grasp. Because of their emotional bodies they are complicated. They can't see straight because they can't look straight. They look for problems and miss the simple solution in front of them.

The simple truth here is that your conscious attention, once focused on the inner feeling of yourself, will destroy whatever is false in that feeling. Since emotion or unhappiness is the falsehood in you (because it turns to pain) it is gradually dissolved or destroyed. What is left behind is the true — your joyous, natural, vibrant self, your happy body. This can never be annihilated because it alone is real in you.

As the false is destroyed you come alive.

So let me restate the practical side of this process and take it a little further. Whether you are peaceful, or agitated after a blazing row (and especially if you are upset or angered by anything in this book) sit down and focus your inner attention on the feeling in the area of your navel, and hold it.

Then, when you've got hold of it, sink into it, sink into that feeling. It will try to throw you off, like the momentum of a spinning disc. Stay with it. Lower yourself, your attention, into it. Become it, become the feeling, the sensation. But without thinking.

You do this simply by being still. Stillness is your only strength against the extraordinary opponent within you.

Stiller and stiller is the way.

Only stillness, the stillness of your perception, your conscious awareness undisturbed by thought or consideration, has the power to dissolve the accumulated discontent, pain and restlessness. Stillness alone can get into it, penetrate it.

As you succeed you will feel pain, fear, doubt, and you will feel threatened. These feelings will be old concealed emotions, rising up through you, being dissolved as they are faced up to. The emotional body will writhe, complain, cry, ache and try to scream through your physical body. It will do anything to make you run away, to remove your searing conscious attention from it. It will try to force you to get up and move about, grab a drink or go out. It will try to convince you that you or I are mad, make you give up and declare the whole thing is pointless. But you must hold.

You must hold your body still as long as you possibly can. Then move around if you must; take a break for ten minutes. Then sit down and start again. Do not give up.

When I say 'hold your body still' I do not mean suppress it. It is the cornered emotion that will move your body at these times. By holding the emotion itself, it will be powerless to make your body move. Emotion cannot move while you are focused on it.

The emotional body is a living thing, living off you like a parasite, and it does not want to die. But that is what's happening. You are killing it, killing all your painful and lonely past with your awareness of the present.

Only now is real.

When it gets hard, remember to hold to the good, the true and the right, now. For only now is real.

As you come to the truth of life, your emotional body goes through the tunnel of death. And that can give you a hard time, for a while. Everyone goes through the tunnel of death, sooner or later; consciously or unconsciously. Everyone has to pass through their own resistance — the emotional conditions that have gathered in them, the hate, resentment, impatience, the thought, the wanting and trying; all the deadening material of the emotional body. That is where the idea of hell comes from. You make your own hell, and as you withdraw into yourself you have to meet what you have made. Don't be afraid; it is only your emotional body, only the ignorance that you have gathered.

The way to deal with hell is to be still, to be present. For hell, the ignorance in your past, cannot stand the stillness of your presence. When it is time to die, even in the hardest death, just be still and be where you are. Stillness will get you through.

Love, The Teacher

Love is the point of the pyramid of existence, not part of it.

Love is real. But the love that knows pain is not real.

Real love is pure and natural; it is not selfish and emotional like human love.

Human love is the love that cries over lost objects or persons. Human love is not fulfilling for long. It doesn't last. It brings pain and heartbreak. Human love is not natural.

In a normal upbringing, children quickly lose the natural feeling of the joy of life in the body — the love you are born with. Normal human or emotional love is induced from a very early age, as love and contentment become associated with external conditions, outer confirmations and perceptions of love. So, when a loved object or person is taken away, the child feels it as loss of love. Crying over a broken toy is a demonstration of this. Later in life, the child (as you the adult) will frequently demonstrate the point again. Amidst much weeping and unhappiness, when someone or something you love dies or leaves you, your heartfelt cry will be 'My love is dead. My love has left me. I can't go on'. Which is not the truth. Your love is always within you.

Your love is within, to feel now, precisely as it was when you were a baby alone and gurgling, contented in your cradle. But the exquisite fineness of love is obscured by your dependence since birth on seeing it reflected externally. Because human love is coarse, you have lost your sensitivity to the purity of love. Although at times you will touch it within, and be filled with the wonder of its unknowable energy, you can no longer feel it constantly and consciously. You are unable to take

47

love direct. You want a reflection of it, not love as it is, selfless and pure.

Pure love is unselfish because it doesn't need to take a single thing away from anyone. You can be or feel pure love without needing anyone to be with you; no one else even has to exist. Pure love is utterly undemanding of anything or anyone in the world. It is complete as it is, in you. Being complete and unending, it ensures there's no unhappiness in you to make others unhappy. That is love.

This love will also ensure that conditions and individuals appear outside you to reflect your love, for you to love. Where you are, they will be. But when they go, as all things must, they will not break your heart. Love, the same love within you, will always come again in form.

✳

When you feel love, you feel the beautiful feeling of yourself that you were born with. But as your perception of it is no longer pure, to stir that love you need the stimulation or reflection of somebody or something outside you. Whether the person or object is present or not, the fact is that the love you feel or want is already in you: it is not outside you. Even the love you're going to feel in the future, for someone you've not yet met, is there and can be felt now — if you can be still enough. But from infancy you have been taught not to be still. You have been taught, as a way of life, to leave the beautiful formless love, the stillness within, and project your whole attention out through the senses onto myriads of forms, and myriads of constantly changing connections, not only in the world but in your head or memory. This requires you to be mentally always on the go. With the result that you can't stop thinking, or worrying, even when you want to — unless your mind is engaged in something. Therefore your mind is always on the move: never still.

In your cradle, your entire attention was focused on moving sights and sounds, rattles, colours, faces, dolls and the loving arms of your mother. Your awareness was deflected onto what was happening outside your body. You learned to like the stimulation; looking for and depending on the loving cuddles, eye-catching colours and soft teddy bears. Now, in the adult, the rattles are for real. They have turned into people — people who are seldom ever still, even when they are not moving. They keep you from being still, and you keep them from being still. Stimulation — that's what makes good company. Even when people are not with you they keep you busy, because you keep thinking about them, which makes you feel as though you are feeling them (in a good or bad way, liking or disliking them). Seldom are you still enough to feel your love direct, without some medium in-between.

The difficulty is: people change from the company you like into a person you love. This is because an individual man or woman is the nearest reflection you can get to the image of your love. Your love within is true, still, silent and patiently waiting. But your attraction to what appears as the opposite sex, is your attraction to the sensual image of the other half of your love within, the other half of yourself, which you have projected outside and are now vainly looking to find in some outer form that you like. As you continue to project your attention onto someone (or something) you like, it will turn into attraction, and then love.

This feeling of love starts with liking. If you persist in projecting your liking — by thinking about the person; that is, by giving them your attention when they are not even with you — the liking turns to a feeling of love. When you cannot be with them, the feeling turns to pain — the pain of wanting what you do not have. Parted from your love, you will feel unhappy and you will say love is painful. As day follows night, human love must bring pain.

But the truth is you are not parted from your love. Your love is within, as always. Love does not cause pain. Only ignorance causes pain.

The pain is due to the ignorance of thinking you are separate from your love; and to identifying your love with an image of it. You cry for the mirror, or the reflection in it, instead of being the reality looking into the mirror. You see what is not the truth and suffer from not seeing the truth. No wonder you hurt. It is like dreaming you've lost the top half of your body and are having to search through hundreds of suitcases to find it — when it is obvious you can't be separate from half of yourself, unless you are dreaming.

Human love arises from liking and disliking.

Love is not 'liking'. Love is beyond liking and disliking. It is possible to love someone without liking them. As it is possible to like someone without loving them. Real love is when you neither like nor dislike, yet are not indifferent.

Liking and disliking give rise to human love. Breaking consciously with this love, or dying to your likes and dislikes, is as painful when it happens as losing everything you have ever loved . . . But then, love itself floods in.

You must no longer confuse love with liking. This will start to happen naturally as you read on and begin to see in the reflection of your daily life how dependent you are on the stimulation of liking and disliking.

It is sufficient to see your dependence in the moment it reveals itself. No effort is required.

*

From birth, everyone (including you) is compelled to identify with likes and dislikes and become attached to them. This is encouraged by the ignorance of emotional parents, teachers and society. From the first moment of apparent comprehension, you were taught to 'like this', to 'like that'; to react to stimulation with pleasure or excitement. (At the same time, this stimulation pleases or excites the parent — yesterday's child, still in the making.)

What is not realised is that the child (or adult), in learning to attach itself to the pleasant, excited feeling of what it likes (called 'good') is automatically attaching itself to the opposite — the negative, painful excitation of what it does not like. When the object is removed, the 'good' feeling inevitably comes to an end. This is called 'bad', and the feeling will be registered as depression, anger, frustration, discontent or boredom.

When you embrace what you like, you embrace what you're not going to like in the future.

To the degree that anything you like excites you at any time, you'll have to suffer at a later time the same degree of negative excitement because of something you do not like. Pleasure excited or induced in this way must end in pain; and pain must end in relief of pain, or pleasure. 'Good' must follow 'bad' and 'bad' must follow 'good' as day follows night and night follows day.

Liking and disliking are one entity — as the two ends of a fence are one fence; although, in time, the beginning and end must follow each other, whichever end you start at. Liking and disliking are precisely the same excitement of the emotions; except that one has a plus or positive quality and the other a minus or negative quality. They are the two ends of the same animal; one the tail, relatively harmless, often soft and caressing, and the other the head which bites. Play with the animal and you play with both parts.

The excitement of liking/disliking is identical with the stimulation of pleasure/pain, happiness/unhappiness. They are artificially induced and are actually a device resorted to by humanity as a substitute for the vanishing natural joy of life, one's pure love within. Once you lose the sensitivity to feel the sweetness of life, you have to have a substitute and that's what excitement is. It creates an artificial feeling of life on which everyone gets hooked.

So your whole attention is focused from birth on the artificially stimulated feeling of what in the world pleases you or does not please you. Until finally you succumb to the self-delusion that life or the feeling of being alive is identical with the feeling of liking — 'I feel excitement: I feel alive. Give me more: I feel more life'. In your ignorance, you are unable to perceive the other half of the equation — what's going on in the subconscious. Here the awareness is: 'When I feel pleasure, I feel alive. And when I feel pain, I also feel alive. Good and bad — both give me the feeling of life. At this level, I don't care whether it is pleasure or pain that I feel. All that matters is that I feel alive'.

But what about the tears on the surface? The wailing, the plea for relief and the protest, 'I do not want this unhappiness'.

No one wants to be unhappy, do they?

Yes. They do.

When you are unhappy you want to be unhappy.

Otherwise you would not be unhappy. You cannot blame anyone or anything else. The unhappiness is in you and it's yours.

The truth is you love your unhappiness. You won't let it go. You cling to it.

Your love of unhappiness is your love of the world — your attachment to what you like and dislike in it. When you are unhappy it's always about something in the world, even if it is only your worldly dislike of yourself. While you still love the world, you are attached to it through your likes and dislikes. You cannot feel the much finer love of life within you; not enough to give up the attachment. So you go on needing the excitement of its pleasure and pain.

You cannot love life and the world. It is one or the other. Love of the world will obscure the love of life. When you no longer need the world's pain you won't need its phoney pleasure either. You will have the natural joy of life that never ends. You will no longer be dependent on the world's up-and-down excitement.

And yet the world will not vanish. You will still be in it. You will still do what you do and enjoy what you do. But you will not be attached to it. You will perform better in it because you won't be unhappy. You will be able to love more. And it will no longer have the power to hurt you.

✳

The truth, for you to see in your own daily experience from this moment on, is that just as you are happy to be happy, you are happy to be unhappy — because that's the only way you can feel alive (in your present though waning ignorance).

Happy to be unhappy!

In between the happiness and unhappiness there is boredom — living death, with no excitation of the liking and disliking, no interplay in the subconscious. But you are only bored because you are ignorant of the truth and have lost the natural feeling of the life in yourself. You no longer feel life within unless stimulated from without, so you feel dead.

Two common extremes of emotional excitement demonstrate this misunderstanding of life, and lack of touch with reality. The exclamations, in moments of intense pleasure, 'This is life! Now I'm really living!' And in moments of similarly intense depression, 'Life is too painful. I'd sooner die'. You might even take poison or a knife to your body in order to prove the point.

Yet even while the want is to die, the joy of life you were born with is still there. Underneath the wretched need for excitement at any price is the joy that makes the birds sing; the joy that despite your unhappy wanton self, never ends.

When it comes, love will teach you — to be what you are.

When you no longer confuse love with the interaction of liking and disliking, you will no longer be looking for love to excite or stimulate you. Then you will find love in person, or love will find you, as surely as the sun shines uninterruptedly beyond the earthly illusion of night and day.

Love will come to you without your looking for it. Suddenly, it will be there. But at first it may not move you, let alone attract you. For a while you may not even notice it. Why would you, when you have only just learned to notice what you like or do not like?

Love is always recognisable by the absence of choice in it. It comes, it happens and it is happening . . . and sometimes because you cannot like it or dislike it, you cannot believe it's happening . . . and yet you see it happening. You cannot choose love as you would choose a bride or a lover. Love chooses you. And there is no mistake.

But if you are still too deeply attached to liking and disliking, you will see and want some choice in what love brings; you will react from there in the same old way and it will teach you nothing but the lesson the chooser never learns: pleasure always turns to pain.

Love is joy and joy has no opposite.

You may not be able to say that you like what love brings. But you will not be able to say that you dislike it either. It will be right. And that will be sufficient for you.

First, love will teach you how to love yourself. It will do this by compelling you to give up disliking and liking yourself. You will lose that choice. And you will feel like you are dying.

It will then teach you not to like or dislike where you are. You will lose that choice too. And you will feel that you are dead.

All this will seem like pain, not like love. But while it lasts, the pain will only be your choosing to hold on to some object or image of love and not love itself. In your pain or ignorance you may choose to leave love, to have what you like (along with what you don't like) for another round of time. But love will always come again in the same choiceless way.

Finally, when you are ready, when your likes and dislikes have lost most of their substance, love will provide the choiceless opportunity for you to serve love with your life so that you never have to choose or want again.

✻

The daily pain, conflict and confusion of the world is the unconscious interaction of likes and dislikes.

The daily pain, conflict and confusion of the spiritual way is the conscious dying to them.

You must die consciously to your likes and dislikes, to your attachment to them.

This is the hardest death of all.

Only when the attachment to your likes and dislikes is dissolved for all time, can you *be* — be what you are. This is the end of existence as a burden.

The spiritual process of detachment from your likes and dislikes requires you to hear and understand the enormity of what you are dealing with, at every level of yourself and your existence. And it requires you to apply that understanding to the reality of your daily life moment to moment, within and without, as your own self-knowledge.

Reading this book, which is all about yourself, is that process.

*

Likes and dislikes are the fluctuating feelings that sit on top of the awareness of the natural feeling of life — the unwavering joy or bliss of being alive, or simply being.

People make the error of thinking they are in this state by just being their normal self. They overlook the intermittent depressions, moods and problems — the unhappiness — that they voluntarily carry around with them as part of their personal self or normal life.

The state of being is distinguished by being at all times in the joy of life within — no unhappiness. And this is reflected externally by the absence of any problems in the world. As within, so without.

Being is pure sensation. And being in pure sensation is a distinctly blissful, self-sustaining feeling. The original Sanskrit-speaking sages of India called it 'ananda'. It does not vary or end. It is the pure feeling of life as the sensation or perception of yourself free of dependence on the world or attachment to it.

When you feel anything but easy in your sensation you feel the disturbance in the next stratum or level of yourself. Here the sensation is no longer one pure feeling but contains many different, changing feelings. This level of emotion, this substratum, consists of hard-set emotional sediment, a bedrock of all the hurts, disappointments and frustrations you've had since childhood and have not faced up to.

This unhappy core of yourself acts like a gong. It reverberates with the emotional interplay — the excitement, good and bad — of your likes and dislikes, which you register as changing feelings or moods.

As this stratum of yourself lies under the surface, in your subconscious, the only parts of it that show and which you can consciously get hold of and deal with in your daily life, are its two opposing poles — your liking and your disliking. If you watch closely and are still enough, you will see that these stick up in your awareness; like two harmless-looking mountain peaks. They are always there; but they have become so much the scenery of yourself that you don't notice them any more, let alone know them or feel them to be intrusive or menacing.

They are in fact seething volcanoes; although they give no overt sign of the force of unhappiness that links them underneath and periodically explodes, making your life a misery, or someone else's life a misery through you.

Let me ask you a question that most people have pondered on at some time or other. How did individual Nazi men and women muster sufficient inhumanity to inflict such unspeakable atrocities on their completely helpless victims? Or the Japanese on their equally helpless prisoners-of-war? Or any other national or partisan group, on any other helpless group of people or individuals? How are any of us able to inflict on one another and other life-forms the cruelties that all are guilty of?

All violence, hatred and inhumanity arise from that subconscious stratum of old ingrained personal pain and falsehood, the unhappiness that is in everyone.

The Child Possessed

EVERY CHILD IS BORN WITH LOVE as the feeling of itself. That is why a baby, without any external stimulation, will lie staring into space, gurgling happily or blissfully in the sensation of its own natural joy or being within its body. The baby's irresistible and delightful smiles express the constant bliss of the true self that it is feeling. It would continue to be consciously in touch with this feeling for the rest of its days but for the ignorance of its parents and society.

The parents, in ignorance of their own true self and therefore of the true self of the child, set out as quickly as possible to draw it lopsidedly out of itself towards their own unhappy, confused and lopsided condition. With the assistance of other misguided family members, they do this by focusing the infant's entire attention onto the sound of rattles, the sight of moving colours and twitching faces, the feeling of fabric dolls and the physical pressure of a loving squeeze — all of which deflect the baby's awareness from the constancy of the joy of life within to the passing stimulation of what happens to be happening outside. Very rarely is there any conscious affirmation, acknowledgement or participation in the child's precious inner state or consciousness. This, by omission and neglect, dies on the vine.

Gradually, the nursery and family routine induces in the child recognition and then reliance on these artificially stimulated feelings of what happens to please it or not please it in the outer world. It forgets its true self and, by becoming unconscious of it, leaves it. It begins looking for sensory excitement as a way of living. When there's no one around to shake the rattle, make funny faces or excite the child —

when what pleases it is missing — it has less and less inward joy to fall back on. The child becomes increasingly discontented, lonely and unhappy. It becomes emotional and demanding; wanting without knowing what it wants.

Originally the child was content to be with its own love within, given that its natural physical needs were met. But now it requires constant and increasing reassurance — emotional love, the outer world's hot-and-cold substitute for real love. (Mother love, though not always reliable, is the best of this.) The child that was spiritually individual and free, is now emotionally dependent, an emotional captive of the world, a miniature carbon-copy of the rest of the unhappy human race.

*

If you are a parent and truly love your child you will make it your selfless, loving responsibility to keep the child in contact with its original consciousness and the sweet feeling of itself. The child needs to feel the firm and loving embrace of the mother and father or guardian as often as possible. But physical love is not enough; there must be intelligence in it. From the first moment the new-born baby lies in your arms, speak directly to it in straightforward language and loving tones. Speak to it about the wonder and knowledge of life and love, and about keeping unhappiness out of yourself. Speak about what you have discovered from reading this book and from applying the truths of it in your daily life. Speak from your own self-knowledge, your integrity.

As you practise addressing the child in this way, you will find it becomes increasingly easy to maintain an intelligent and meaningful communication. It might seem like a monologue at first, but gradually you will realise that it is an extraordinary dialogue. From its inner selfless consciousness, its love, the child is silently responding to every word.

Mothers naturally tend to speak like this with their new-born. But because of the mothers' unhappiness, and due to our material times and the lack of real knowledge of life and love, the expression is no longer conscious enough or real enough to be sustained.

You must understand that the communication I am describing is energetic. It is not dependent on words, although the sound of your words will actually carry the conscious speechless energy of your love. And this communicates direct to the child's consciousness or love.

It won't be long before the child begins to use words, and then you can speak together about the truth of life and love that you've found within and without. The child's frontal awareness, and its perceptions of the world without, will then be in tune with the energy of its real self within. Then its development will not be lopsided.

Continue the dialogue throughout the child's life. It will have much to say that will utterly astound you. You will find it responding from an amazing place within, far more real and profound than its years. You will grow in love and truth together. That is what parenthood and childhood are for.

*

In a normal upbringing, when the child first starts to talk, the unhappiness seated in the subconscious rises and gains a recognisable ascendancy. Likes and dislikes begin speaking through the child. The one who smiled and gurgled in the crib, the same delightful, self-contented child speaks; and then the other restless, unhappy thing speaks. Both are using the same body. But only one is real.

The parents and closest adults, by conversing with the child's likes and dislikes, by entertaining them with false notions of love and kindness, give the invading emotion human status or recognition. This is disastrous. The likes and dislikes start to assume an independent emotional identity and a false authority. This is centred in the throat.

Unsuspected by all, because it is the norm, the child is being taken over. It is being emotionally possessed; psychically possessed. Inevitably and tragically, the parents accept or tolerate the degenerate emotion as part of the child. From its seat in the throat, the emotion gradually invades every cell in the body. It is a slow process, greatly accelerated and strengthened by puberty.

The child itself is powerless to resist the psychic invader. Its one hope is to have the support, strength and authority of parents or guardians whose absence of unhappiness has made their love real enough. Due to our times this is extremely rare. But there is more chance of it happening now — through you.

Parents who are sufficiently one with their own life and love can stand fast. They can be surrogate for the child and consciously face the emotion. This is not a fight or battle with the child, although it might be perceived as one. It is done by pure presence, by confronting the unhappy psychic invader with the only authority it will yield to or cannot bear — an utterly unemotional, unexcitable presence of love. This is love beyond acquisition or human understanding. It is love free of the distractions of liking and disliking; selfless love.

As things are in the world, however, the emotion in the child is invariably faced with human love — love dependent on the stimulation of external perceptions, good and bad. This love is itself emotional. It gets sucked into a psychic vortex and contributes to the force of the possession through its own psychic possession. It does not have the essential endurance, the power to resist; so it compromises with the invader, usually in the name of 'love'. The result is that the growing child's habitual declarations and posturings of what it likes and does not like, what it wants and does not want, although at times infuriating to its loving elders, are quietly accepted, for better or for worse, as a perfectly normal, tolerable and intolerable, contradictory human self.

The child is shaping up nicely to take its place in the rest of the perfectly normal, tormented and tormenting unhappy world. In later life, this automatic acceptance of the child's contradictory self into the human fold will inevitably create problems for it, and for society. But as everyone is living the same way, who is to say it is contradictory?

For example, when the emotion or liking of patriotism excites him (or her) to go and kill someone for his country, he will be praised and his action highly commended. But when the same emotion of liking or disliking excites him to kill or injure someone at another time, he will be censured and locked up; or in emotionally assertive societies, executed. He will never really get over the confusion of such contradictory justice. But he will try to live with it for better and for worse; as society will try to live with him.

The young child's original, fine, inner feeling of sweet self-fulfilment is disappearing under the crude weight of acquired excitability, impatience and discontent. Coming in fast are the frustrations and anxieties of wanting what it likes but cannot have, and not wanting what it has. The periods in which it can 'just be', alone and without entertainment, are shorter and fewer.

To feel that it is alive, the child now has to like or not like what it's doing, instead of simply being and doing. It especially has to feel the excitement and psychic tension that is created in the presence of others by declaring what it likes and dislikes.

If you are a responsible parent or teacher you will not converse with the child's likes and dislikes. You will not allow the child to say what it likes or does not like. You will guide it to find other words to express preferences, so that the selfish force of liking/disliking does not get expression through the voice (through the wilful throat centre). You will not allow the exclamations 'I want' or 'I don't want'. You will have no discussion with the wanting or not-wanting energy.

You will not do any of this by force or suppression. Yet you will be able to punish the child as necessary; explaining to it (when it is still and receptive) what both of you are confronting, precisely what you are doing, and how. This alone produces enduring trust and authority.

If you have been contributing your wisdom and consciousness to the child since birth, as I suggested earlier, it will not be shocked by what you are doing and why it is being done. In fact, the child will be your collaborator. For you will have informed it long ago of the one and only danger that faces all human beings coming into existence. It will know all about the psychic invader and much of what is in this book. You will have demonstrated it in the child's own experience — the most powerful instruction possible. But the longer you have left it, the harder it's going to be.

*

A distinct, intermittent ugliness creeps into the child. When the ugliness is there, even the most devoted parent finds it hard to believe that this is the offspring they love and gave birth to. The child scowls. It frowns. Darkness is there. It grimaces, defies and wilfully ignores. Cunning appears in the eyes. The look sometimes is so old, so knowing of its own perversity, that it is impossible to reconcile it with a child.

The ferocity of the unhappiness is sometimes diabolical. The child demands; emotionally, senselessly, mindlessly. It screams, red-faced with rage, working itself up into near hysteria. It writhes, rolls its eyes, as if demented. And occasionally you can catch its sly, detached and knowing glance looking out to confirm that it's getting the emotional reaction it wants, and feeds off, from anyone in the vicinity.

It lives off reaction. Sympathy, anger, sentiment, disgust, repulsion; any emotion at all will satisfy and nourish it so that in its own good time it will be free to rise again. The force of its unhappiness is pitiless; unmerciful to both child and parent.

The child is left exhausted afterwards, drained and unable to comprehend what happened to it, apart from perhaps its memory of the helpless parent's anger or fury.

The ugliness, when it is there, exploits patience, tolerance and love. It actually wants punishment, and the raw experience of it, so it inflames others and gets what it wants. It drives mother and father to a violence of mood or action that they never believed they were capable of. Then again it howls and screams because it wants what it does not have — this time an end to the punishment.

What it does not have, it wants. What it does have, it does not want. Nothing can pacify or satisfy it. It demands love and understanding and crucifies love and understanding. It injects guilt like venom into those who react to it: and despair into those who would try to comfort or heal it. It does not know what it wants because it already has what it wants, its self. It is pure unhappiness.

It is that which likes-and-does-not-like, coming into existence once again to make life on earth a misery. This fiendish force is the living emotion, the living intelligence of psychic unhappiness, that enters and possesses every infant through the ignorance of the world. And it lives in the subconscious of every man and woman until rooted out by conscious confrontation.

No one knows that every child is being psychically possessed, because everyone who could know are themselves psychically possessed. Occasionally, people vaguely perceive the psychic possession in others. But the full extent of it, the enormity of it, cannot be comprehended until the individual has cleared his or her own psychic space of the invading evil. Only then is the man or woman spiritually or consciously strong enough to face the awful truth:

The whole world is psychically possessed.

You must learn to recognise the first sign of emotion rising to express itself in the child. This will be a seemingly harmless word, reaction or gesture. At that moment you must immediately confront both child and emotion, alerting the child to what is coming (mood or unhappiness), and to be ready for it.

Your approach must always be that you are doing it together. 'We will not have it in us, will we?' And although the failures seem almost incessant, you must keep going. For if you are going to save the child, you must also save yourself — by keeping the mood and unhappiness out of yourself.

You must be firm and strong; patient, present, emotionless and wise. Remember, there is no failure for either the child or yourself: just endeavour to do better next time and don't dwell on the past. The child has to be led to see the invader for what it is — something separate from itself, an unhappy emotion that the happy, untroubled child does not want and therefore will not hold on to.

＊

The psychic possession of the growing child continues, unsuspected. The descent into ignorance and unhappiness is fostered throughout by family life, with its celebration of birthdays, Christmas, anniversaries, with gift-giving and constant fuelling of the child's expectation of future pleasure and reward. Family life insidiously affirms and dignifies an identification with the invading false self.

Through the example and indulgence of parents, the child learns to state and restate what it likes and does not like — supposedly genuine expressions of itself — and learns to defend and justify these acquired posturings with righteous, outraged vehemence. It learns from example to accept that the strife and unhappiness this causes is normal, and even necessary to family life; necessary to love. Most unfortunate of all, it learns from elders to believe that it has the right to be unhappy, moody and ill-tempered; that as these are natural to human beings so they can be forgiven or excused in oneself.

The parents continually demonstrate their almost complete dependence on liking and disliking as a way of life. Their main topics of conversation and most memorable experiences are based on what they like and do not like. The child is continuously exposed to conversations like this:

— 'Did you have a good time' (exciting, get-what-you-like time) 'on the holiday you were looking forward to' (for excitement)?

— 'Yes, interesting' (not so exciting). 'But depressing when . . .' (negatively exciting). 'How have you been?'

— 'We've been well' (meaning physically well; no mention of love of the beauty or truth of life). 'But John's unhappy about his job' (negatively excited). 'He had a wonderful promotion' (exciting) 'but then . . .'

— 'What did you do yesterday?' (The questioner looks for excitement, not love or life).

— 'Nothing much' (no excitement). 'But tonight we're having a dinner party . . .' (Excitement to look forward to, and more conversations like this one about likes and dislikes).

Apart from the influence of their friends, the parents' attachment to the possessing psychic entity is kept alive and vibrant by society's relentless stimulation of likes and dislikes. This is done through the exciting propaganda of advertising agencies, along with the likes and dislikes (opinions of what is emotionally and sensationally meaningful) of the news, information and entertainment media. In daily life there is virtually no reference whatsoever to the joy of just being alive without the stimulation or excitement of some activity or problem. The whole waking life of child, family and society is directed towards artificially generating the excitement of liking or pleasure; or stimulating the (exciting) fear of losing it.

Drinks, food, music, recreation, fashion, furnishings, religious beliefs, personality, nursery stories, books, films, friends, associates are all chosen on the basis of who or what stirs or might stir the feeling of liking or pleasure. And the threatened loss of these things excites the opposite feeling of dislike or displeasure. (Gambling, competition and even secret love affairs owe their attraction to the exciting stimulus of possible loss, as much as possible gain.)

And so the child continually absorbs into its subconscious the parents' own underlying unhappiness. The psychic possession perpetuates itself. And the parents don't know what to do to undo what they've done.

*

If the child (as an adult) is to be freed of unhappiness and confusion, a more real parent or guardian will come along, point the way and do what the original parents and guardians could not do. This is the teacher of truth.

His presence and words will cause a good deal of pain. In adulthood the possessing psychic entity is well and truly entrenched — as the unhappy, contradictory personality itself. In fact and truth, the pain is its destruction.

The pain that is suffered, and the disruption that occurs in the life to bring about the pain, will be in proportion to how much the individual longs to be free. As will be the floodings of joy, wonder and love that occur in between the periods of suffering.

Longing is not wanting. Everybody wants to be free, but few long for it. Wanting has innumerable objects. But longing is for life, for freedom which has no object. You just long for what you do not know and cannot name.

The teacher of truth is surrogate for the head of the human family, the one parent, the one God or one life or good that knows no unhappiness in time, and whose joy it is that you should real-ise this in yourself, as yourself.

*

Everything is centred on the physical body, the senses and their functions. In childhood the identification starts with what is happening to the child's own body or person. Then it extends to what is happening to others and eventually to the whole world. Useless involvement, useless curiosity and hypocritical concern increase in proportion to the growing number of things, people and conditions there are to like or dislike.

Stimulation, good or bad; kicks all the way. Tears alternate with laughter, excitement with depression. And finally, as it all began in the initial pleasure (or pain) of birth and hope, so it all ends in the final pain and disappointment (or relief) of death.

Poets and dreamers, feeling the presence of the one life but never managing to consciously find it, present the contorted living process as something majestic and dignified, when it is an avoidable obscenity — throes of unhappiness artificially induced and imposed upon a whole species through wilful ignorance of itself.

The unchanging reality of bliss in the natural being, and the joy that lies under the acquired excitability, remain unperceived; seldom consciously approached or addressed. Anything that approximates to conscious inner sensation is likely to be limited to sexual, audio-visual, gastronomic or drug-induced stimulation; or to the feeling of physical hunger, physical pain or emotional dejection. For any accidental inner awareness in this society, there is only one resort — the doctor.

The love, the being, the peace of self that absorbs all problems, is unknown.

Society, comprising the entire man-made world, is the working model of universal psychic possession or force. And this in spite of the learned psychiatrists and psychologists who are all unhappy — and therefore possessed.

Old superstitions supported attempts to rid people of evil spirits by various tortures and cures. These were partial perceptions of the truth of possession, but as the perceptions were psychically distorted in the perceivers themselves, the truth of universal possession was not seen. The 'evil' was perceived in others, not in oneself. If occasionally the possession was seen in oneself (which is the first real step towards eliminating it) the individual invariably regarded it as a sign of his or her own madness.

But who am I? The madness I see in me; or I who am perceiving the madness in me?

Accepting the madness as oneself, and not the perceiver, was the error. And today, again due to the psychic distortion inherent in all, this same mistake continues to be the main impediment to seeing the truth, living it, and then being it.

Another fact, which also applies today, was that apparently no one free enough of psychic possession was around to inform the sufferer of the truth and thus help him or her to free themselves. Intellectualising or rationalising the possessing emotional energy has debunked the old 'evil spirit' approach and made it unpopular. But in no way has it reduced the actuality and reality of the psychic possession of everyone. Despite learned and professional rationalisations, the almost total psychic possession of the human race continues unabated. And it is reflected in the universal unhappiness of every man and woman — expressing itself as worry, fear, argument, heartbreak, doubt, violence, guilt, loneliness, lack of love, poverty, exploitation, business, and war in any name or form.

The rational and scientific mind might accept the term 'emotional possession' as a description of someone who is angry, jealous or seething with hatred. But it does not perceive that this emotional possession is psychic possession — possession by something not oneself. To the rational, scientific mind the word 'psychic' with its connotation of non-physical influence, is a bit too close to the truth — that man is possessed by a sinister force, not far removed from the old evil spirits. So the word 'psychic', like the expression 'evil spirits' before it, has to be rationalised for everyone's rational acceptance, watered down to the less meaningful, less direct word, 'emotion'.

To avoid any misunderstanding and distortion of what I am saying by the rational mind, let me repeat the point: to be psychically possessed is to have unhappiness in your life.

If you have unhappiness in yourself or your life at any time, you are psychically possessed.

The Word of the World

THE WORLD TODAY is run, not by the leaders of the various nations who appear to have control, but by The Unhappy Supermind — the super-normal, super-rational analysing mind. This is the amazing and clever intelligence of the psychic force of unhappiness that has possessed mankind through the child and through the subconscious; and which sustains the possession through human attachment to unhappiness and the past.

The Supermind is merely mental and emotional, therefore loveless and lifeless. It is taking the life and love out of the human race.

The mental part of the Supermind controls the thinking side of every single person, as the emotional part controls the feeling side. The mental part is seated in everyone's memory, making them think and talk about the past; and the emotional part is seated in the sentiments and attachments of everyone's likes and dislikes, making them live off their feeling of the past.

In yourself, the loveless and lifeless working of the mind is immediately recognisable. The mind can only *think* about love and life. It cannot be love and life now.

So the mind is distinguished by being unhappy about love and life. Whenever you are unhappy about love and life, that's the mind at work. And when the mind is unoccupied it must remain unhappy because it cannot be absence of unhappiness (love and life) for only you can be that. So the mind *thinks* about love or life and *feels* unhappy, or it gets emotional about love and life. This makes it *think* and *feel* that something is missing on earth or in the world and that in

69

order to try and find what's missing whatever exists has to be changed.

So, in its unhappiness, and searching for what it can never find because it can never be, the Supermind moves people and nations around, ceaselessly changing all that exists in the world, without ever getting any closer to love and life. It is the cleverest and most forceful thing in existence. But because it can never be the truth, never be love and life, it is utterly ignorant, utterly unhappy, self-perpetuating and ultimately, in its terrible unhappiness, self-destructive.

In its search for what it can never find, the super-rational Supermind every day takes mankind further away from a feeling contact with blessed life on blessed earth; seducing men, women and children into a sterile, electronic (mentalised) existence, further away from the ever-present love within. The children are vanishing into imagined worlds of space where there is no blessed life or love at all. And the adults lose themselves in a world dependent on electromagnetic and ultra-clever computerised and mentalised gadgetry, calling that lifeless and loveless world 'life'.

The women are dying for love; but don't know it or they would be able to do something about it. And the men, seduced and reduced by the love of technology, are dying for life as they disappear headfirst into meaningless inventions and devices.

Man, woman and child are either elated, bored or depressed; depending on which button the mind happens to be pushing, or not pushing.

*

So the super-rational analysing mind — your mind — is the architect of our loveless and material times. And one of its chief destructive activities is the degradation of language, all human languages.

First it takes the communication value (the life) out of key words. These are the words originally formulated by the race to express the beauty and joy of life on earth and within. Five such words are love, peace, beauty, life and truth.

Each key word represents a state of being. When the language was young and vital, and before the unhappy mind was able to degrade it, the actual sensation of the state of being of the person using the word was evoked in the hearer. No one used a word that did not represent themselves at that moment.

Language then was not a mental process as it is today. Dictionaries describing the meanings of words would have been impossible. Words were actually sounds that ran together like wordless songs. The sound alone communicated the sensation. Language was more like birdsong. But due to the mind's unhappy activities, mansong — the song of life made conscious — degenerated into wordsong, chanting, mantras and speech.

In our loveless, material times, the method used by the mind to degrade the language is the repetition of a word by every mind. This senseless (feeling-less or state-less) repetition destroys the true-life feeling that created the word-sound, leaving behind a purely mental function — an empty word, a rational noise signifying next to nothing.

This cerebral process removes the consciousness from the word, knocks the living daylights out of it. For instance, the mind has cerebralised the living feeling out of the word 'love'.

Normal daily life (your life) consists of completely meaningless expressions: 'How are you, love? . . . Thank you, love . . . I love my car . . . I love my cat. . . I love this dress. . . I love that!' And other dubious ones such as 'I love you'.

And every child learns by copying adults . . . 'I love dancing . . . I love school . . . I love my teddy bear'.

Not surprisingly, many men and women today are not sure what the word 'love' means. They feel the reality of love within, but the word love as used and demonstrated in living is no longer true; it's just too phoney, no longer adequate to express the sweet intimacy, immediacy and vitality of the pure passion for life that they feel.

The unconscious masses of the people vainly attempt to communicate the feeling of love — giving gifts and writing nice-sounding sentences with empty words to communicate the one true and simple feeling of love that is only in the being of love, the being of the word, and not in the utterance or inscribing of it.

Through senseless repetition the word love has lost its conscious connection with the supreme joy of love or life now, in the individual using it. It stands for wavering attachment, self-gratifying sentiment and an emotion that is not love at all; or for casual convenience and mutually-agreed deception. With the result that the real thing is suffocated in the individual, whose only alternative is to indulge in romantic notions or lustful thoughts. The frustration and unhappiness of living without the reality of love grows and grows.

*

Having removed the living truth from the word, the senseless mind is forced to use other devalued words to make up for the missing integrity of the original word; which of course doesn't work. So the dictionaries grow fatter, the learned discussions longer, and the computer memory-banks more necessary.

While the truth of life, which is vital communication between people, grows less, the mind or unhappiness is served; and insincerity is the smiling practice and posture of the day.

Into the senseless mind's rational shredder have gone all the other meaningful words. And all have come out the other end as practically empty ciphers, fit to serve only the mind's particularity, its likes and dislikes, or its fanciful imagination of what's important.

Life — the unpossessable, immediate, simple sweetness of being of the earth, that is the substance of man's ever-present immortality: mistaken for 'living', the form of life-without-purpose that is pain and living death.

Peace — the ceaseless state of man's inner vital life, available now to all: tragically identified with the outer peace-less, normal condition of living in-between wars and arguments.

Beauty — ever-present within oneself: unhappily thought to be in the object outside that decays, dies or passes in time.

Truth — 'What is truth?' said Pilate. Truth is disguised in all as the lie that suits today's self-interest.

'How do you do? . . . Pleased to meet you . . . Excuse me . . . Good-bye . . . Have a nice day . . . Thank you. You're so kind. I'm

obliged . . . Good morning . . . How are you? . . . Good night! . . .
Dear Ms Smith . . . Yours sincerely/Yours faithfully . . .'

Every expression to describe the beauty and wonder of individuals
interacting, is converted by the love-less mind into a dead, habitual
and formal exercise.

*

Science, business, industry and technology — the wonders of the
age — are the latest expressions of the super-rational Supermind. They
are not concerned with the truth. They are concerned only with what
is true.

What is true is not the truth.

What is true changes in time, according to circumstances. The
truth — love, life, beauty, peace — never changes.

It is true that man has legs. But that is not the truth. Because not
all men have legs. Some lose their legs in time. And the contradiction
or qualification is then true: man has legs, but that particular man
does not have legs. In the truth, there is no contradiction or
qualification.

Science, business, industry, technology, and the information media
which publicise these activities, deal in the particular and what is true
keeps changing according to a particular pursuit or liking. The truth of
science, business, industry, technology and the media is that
everything worthwhile in life is in the future (or the past) and does not
exist now: so it has to be pursued. Each pursuit is a movement, never
an achievement, never an end in itself, as the truth is.

The pursuit of all pursuits is called progress.

Progress is the overall movement, or aberration, of the rational
mind. As what is worthwhile — love, life, beauty, peace and truth —
already is, and never changes, all movement or pursuit has to be a
movement away from it. So science, business, industry, technology
and the media — representing the great movement of progress — each
day take man further and further away from the truth of himself.

The movement is towards what might be true in the future, but which will still change in the particular, making the next movement, the next action, the next aberration, compulsively and unarguably necessary. This truth-less, restless fixation makes all men the slaves of progress.

Progress is merely the frantic flight from truth and the love of escapist emotions, expressed through the loveless, materialistic, progressive mind (the world).

No movement is necessary to find the truth. No movement is possible in truth. There is nowhere to go, nothing to be achieved. Love, life, beauty, peace and truth are now. They are you, now, behind the seductive movement or restlessness of your rational, progressive mind.

Through science, business, education, government, industry, technology and the media, the unhappy Supermind is taking the life and love out of the people and the language at an unprecedented rate. The plummeting descent towards the extinction of life and humanity, or the need of any real language or people at all, has never been so blatantly obvious.

Man exists on this planet only to communicate life and love as the truth or being of himself. Once he ceases to do this, the justification for his existence ends.

Language is communication and people are communication. The people of the earth at any time are as real as what they talk about or communicate. The question at any time is: what are they communicating? Or: what am I communicating with my life? As far as 'they' are concerned you can get the answer by watching the News tonight. For yourself the question is: 'Does my life communicate self-knowledge or the joy of life? Or am I communicating some notion of life or a knowledge that I've picked up or learned in my occupation, and which I ignorantly regard as my life's purpose?'

The scientist, businessman, official, industrialist, educationalist, technologist or media person cannot communicate love and life because their activities are not concerned with love and life, not concerned with the truth. They are concerned with degraded knowledge and with experience outside themselves: both of which lead to self-doubt, loneliness and confusion — lack of love and life —

for themselves and for all those they influence.

Just as no one can talk about their likes or dislikes without their unhappiness or unreality talking through them, so no man or woman can communicate the truth or reality of themselves through their profession or occupation — the medium of life they have chosen for avoiding the truth within. The expertise or knowledge talking through them will have been acquired and is not themselves. What they say or do to serve their occupation will have no love or life in it — no reality. These people (which is all people) will talk about everything except the truth of life and love. They will talk about a subject outside of what they are now. Their words will refer to the past or future, or the present related to some object or condition, but not to 'the now' that is the wonder and the truth of being life now.

What learned and knowledgeable people say may be true in some particular, somewhere, or at some other time, but it will not be the truth of you or life now. So it will sophisticate, complicate and corrupt. Each time the scientist, official or expert utters or repeats what he (or she) thinks is true, the language he uses is made more lifeless for himself and everyone using it. And to the degree that the man believes what he's saying is the truth, or identifies himself with it as a way of life, he makes himself more lifeless, along with all who believe him or even listen to him. As a result both he and everyone else have to find a little more stimulation (good or bad) to feel alive. So life as living becomes ever more complicated, never enough without needing more.

Every moment of every day in the frantic unhappy world this process goes on gaining momentum. Nothing but the truth can restrain it. But there is not enough truth in the world — too few real individuals, or real words.

The truth is only as powerful, as real, as the word. That is, it is only as powerful as the life of the individual man or woman. For finally, man is the word.

Man is the original word.

This is the ultimate truth of yourself. It is described in the opening of the New Testament Gospel of John: In the beginning was the Word and the Word was with God and the Word was God. In him (the Word) was life. And the Word was made flesh.

This does not refer to a distant, historical saviour or any other life. It refers to you, man, the life and the love that you are, the man or woman that you are, freed of your unhappiness. And like all saviours, you must first save yourself.

As the original word, man (or sound) degenerated in time in the mind, so the degeneration, corruption or complication proliferated into innumerable sounds and words called languages, and into myriads of men called the masses. As living symbols of the truth on earth, man and woman, like living words of the truth, have no other meaning or purpose in existence but to express the truth of life as the truth of themselves. Their meaning is their purpose.

The only occupation in living is to find this truth or purpose within. Consequently, through the darkness and confusion of the occupations chosen for them by the rational mind and its emotion, all men and women crave to find the meaning, the purpose of life — which is simply to be, to express the man or woman they truly are now, freed of the mind and its unhappy occupations.

But the mind will not allow this. Each day it continues to drain the language (and the people) of more life and truth. So each day the words (and the people) are multiplied to represent even less truthfully what is true today; because what was true yesterday has already changed and must be redefined, redescribed and re-reported. The jargon, ciphers, graphics, illustrations, lists, discussion, meetings, agendas, conferences, talks and useless information posing as news and informed opinion, every bit of it based on someone's likes or dislikes, on their unhappiness, pours out in an appalling torrent from the printed pages, mailboxes, electronic screens, magnetic speakers and the multiple banks of barren, senseless brains behind them.

Little does the super-rational mind realise that this gigantic descending stream is a repeat in a different time and a different medium of the deluge that wiped out the Ancient World; a modern flood of blind ignorance that will destroy all that man thought was true but was not the truth.

A Political History of the World

The history of mankind is the evolution of unhappiness.

At the beginning of time the individual man or woman was the ruling authority on earth. There was no emotion in this authority: no past, no likes and dislikes, no unhappiness, no self-interest. Each individual was responsible for himself or herself in a way that is unimaginable today.

There was no concept of the masses. There was no notion of what would be good or not good for others, society and the world or even for oneself. There was only one good.

No good is seen in the future.

The good, the only good, was seen, realised or known now, in the individual. And it was known by the absence of unhappiness in himself or herself. So it was not 'a good' as we think of 'good' today. It could not be given to another or shared with someone who did not have it. That would have been to create another or secondary 'good', a notional (not-existent-now) good.

Everyone was responsible for their own good. It was an utterly individual and just authority. One simply took responsibility *now* for the good — the absence of unhappiness in oneself. And all that followed was naturally right or good.

As anyone or everyone could do it, and did it, no excuse existed for not doing it. Consequently, notions of mass good, social or family good, or even of social equality, had no meaning. If all are equal in the timeless good within, all are equal in the unfoldment in time of the good without. What happens is then right, and known to be right, leaving no place for doubt or unhappiness.

These first terrestrials were free of unhappiness or emotion because they were not identified with the physical animal body — the source of all emotion, all unhappiness. They used the senses to perceive the natural wonder of earthly existence, but were detached from them. They retained the self-knowledge that they were the life or consciousness within the body and behind the senses. And in that self-knowledge they knew that what they perceived through the body — the heavens and the earth — was only a tiny fragment, represented in time, of the timeless universe of life within.

The first terrestrials are you and I now, in a different time.

Man and woman today are almost completely identified with and emotionally attached to the animal body. This means they accept the body's mortal nature as their own, along with its justified fear of death and extremely limited vision of life. This forces them to behave according to the rudimentary psychology of the animal. And that creates problems. The animal body, concealing its vulnerability from itself, finds its comfort and peace of mind in the notion of the masses, in belonging to the herd. This is natural to the animal instincts of the body, but not to the individual man or woman, the consciousness behind the animal body.

When there is identification with the body, individuality vanishes. The original terrestrials, detached from the body although still within it, were individuals. So when the earth was ruled by these people it was not a collective or tribal rule. And it was not rule by one privileged person, chief or king. Each individual ruled; by ruling himself or herself.

There was no place for group responsibility — the misguided attempt to produce a notional, secondary good. Such a divisive and disruptive authority would have been utterly irresponsible. Man and woman's one and only responsibility was to life. And that meant keeping unhappiness, the emotion of the fearful herdal instinct, out of themselves. This required no consultation, no consensus, no division, no decisions, no tomorrows, no time. It was done now.

Being free from unhappiness, each man and woman was the pure joy of life on earth. Conscious of that joy as no instinctive animal can be, each was responsible for the joy on earth of all life, simply by refusing to have unhappiness in himself or herself. For life on earth only suffers from man's unhappiness. When he is joyous within, nothing suffers, including himself.

At that time, all life, though outwardly discrete in myriads of physical forms, was united in man's consciousness and inner sense of responsibility, the endless joy of being himself in such a wondrous existence. He was the timeless consciousness in time; the miracle that is man. In beautiful male and female bodies, he was the flower, the fully conscious head of the stem of all earth's beautiful instinctive species. He felt and perceived his nature as inner joy and bliss; a continuous awareness within him, independent of the physical senses and yet reflected through his senses in every form of nature on exquisite earth. He was indeed sovereign of the earth, the only authority and power required to maintain and preserve the joy of life on it.

Mankind was (and is) in paradise on earth.

He had no desire for exclusivity, no fear; because fear only arises from the herdal fear of the death of the body. So immortality, justice, truth, love, life and the law, were inseparable from the joy and bliss of his nature. Today's society, organised as a necessity to provide a sort of justice, law or truth outside the individual, would have been unthinkable. In fact, thinking had not been thought of. Man and woman did not think, because thought only arises when the natural joy of life is missing: thinking about the past or future only arises from unhappiness.

As within, so without. As each individual was free of conflict and problems within, so life on earth without was free of conflict and problems. Today the whole of society is psychically possessed with unhappiness and lost in the body-consciousness. So everyone has a problem or is a problem. And the whole world is a problem, a mass of

79

problems.

The problem behind it all is choice. Everyone's life is spent trying to choose that which attracts what is liked, and that which keeps away what is not liked. They do not realise what's happening. Their likes and dislikes are assertive reactions of the body's instinctive herdal fear, made self-conscious by the identification of man's consciousness with his body. As the likes and dislikes become more numerous and subtle in everyone's life, so do the choices, the thinking, and the problems.

This increasing subtlety is regarded as cultural progress. But really it is the pointless and uncalled-for sophistication of the animal instincts, their evolution or expansion being forced along by the identification of the immortal consciousness with a mortal body.

This sophistication created the notional fear of other herds (other nations) and led to the development of the Bomb and other genocidal weapons. More recently it engendered a contradictory notion; a global concern for the safety of the whole herd of humanity, the masses, now endangered by the same thermonuclear devices that were previously intended as deterrents.

The two opposing notions of what is good — survival of humanity or survival of myself — tear at men and women relentlessly, dividing them in themselves and in society. Since the animal body cannot know the one and only good, it has to continuously chase after countless secondary, notional 'goods', which can never be realised because they exist only in unhappiness.

*

Unhappiness is the evolution of a thing wholly sinister and alien to life on earth. The thing does not exist: it achieves its existence in individual men and women, through their unconscious identification with the body.

Something alien came to earth.

The thing is extracosmic — from outside the immediate cosmos that mankind is involved in. To the reality of our cosmos it is an inferior parasite. And yet its existence through man and woman has created the psychic world of life after death and has degraded their original freedom and pristine spiritual state. There is no death (and never was) but it has created the illusion and fear of death and therefore the need of its opposite, an existence after death.

For man and woman to get back to the original, pure state of life beyond the existence of unhappiness, they have to repossess the psychic realm — their own subconscious or psyche where unhappiness is lodged. They must do this while alive, by consciously entering their subconscious and ridding it of the invading parasite.

The process starts in your own experience with the awareness of the thing's existence in you, and how it works.

The alien is time and thought itself.

The extracosmic alien appears in the mind, every mind, as attachment to time. This manifests as age, as cause and effect and as the evolutionary and historic principle. Thus, it expresses itself in any logical development linking the past with the present.

The alien is the thinker in man, the reasonable man or woman.

It is completely false. It is false because it compels man and woman to reason and believe that the present is dependent on the past, or is the outcome of the past. It deludes them into thinking or believing that the original timeless state of unending joy, bliss and freedom can only be achieved in time, and not now. Imprisoned in this past ignorance, they pursue the impossible, striving through unhappiness to be free of unhappiness; and depending on time to be free of time.

The alien is in everything thought or felt. It is in everything apart from the awareness of bliss within or natural joy without object. In that perception alone are man and woman free of the alien. That awareness is always now, timeless.

Before the alien gained its existence, there was no time, no interval. Everything was and is, now. Man perceived the beauty or reality of the earth direct, through his awareness now, the eternal now within him. So there was no self-consciousness, no self-interest, no ignorant and unhappy subconscious to provide the notion of time, reflection, past or the continuity of existence — no psychic world between mankind and the beautiful earth. Everything was and is immediate, discontinuous, ever new — the eternal consciousness of the earth itself, present in man's perception, as man's perception.

With no past existence or subconscious between the earth and the eternal, there was no evolution. Only when the alien force of time entered man's awareness, and attached him to impressions of the past, did evolution or change start to occur. From then on he started to lose his inner awareness, his one and only good sense, his perception of the one and only good.

As the alien was intolerable to timeless consciousness, it was instantly ejected; so it formed subconsciousness, the human subconscious on top of the timeless consciousness.

However, the alien intelligence had formed an impression in itself, in time, of the timeless sense of the one and only good. As it was only an impression of the good, and not the real thing, it differentiated necessarily into several secondary 'goods', secondary senses which in time appeared as the physical sense organs of hearing, tasting, smelling, seeing and touch-feeling. This manifestation of the senses marked the beginning of the evolution of the species and the externalisation on earth of a physical world.

Thus there are three realms of existence, one on top of the other: eternal consciousness, subconsciousness, and physical consciousness.

It took immense epochs of unhappiness, the suffering of all life in time, to evolve what we now know as the five human sense organs, fixed in the head as the ears, eyes, nose, palate and skin. Like stalks, they emerge from the human brain, itself the product of time, past pain and the same evolutionary trauma that produced all the earth's mortal or sense-perceived creatures.

The earth as we know it, in its familiar shape and form, is also externalised in time. It is the physical externalisation (two levels up) of the pristine terrestrial psyche, the timeless and the changeless — the eternal.

Once externalised through the senses, the earth-image and human psyche entered time and change: and evolution began. Immediately, the manifested earth, representing the previously joyous human psyche, re-enacted with cataclysmic violence the agonising effect of the invasion of unhappiness. The evolutionary evidence of these primordial convulsions and the successive upheavals are preserved today in the dramatic rock formations of the earth's surface. Geological history represents the petrification in stone of the fundamental unhappiness in the human psyche and the existence that came out of it.

The evolution of unhappiness continues to be demonstrated in the earth. Just a few miles below the solid crust, a fiery ocean of molten rock, like the endless unhappiness seething in the tormented human psyche, intermittently boils to the surface with uncontrollable destructive force.

The geophysical evolution or manifestation of the earth is for the time being stable and could be said to be complete. So is the organic evolution of the species that culminated in the human brain and body.

*

When the physical realm was complete, the alien unhappi-ness evolved in a new medium — mankind's unhappy brain with it's fears, doubts, violence, cruelty, greed, loneliness, depression, anger and despair.

The multitudes of emotion in the subconscious were externalised in the people of the earth as the unconscious masses — a massed unconsciousness. As men and women find comfort, excitement and a personal identity in their multitudinous emotions, so they hide from the truth of themselves in the unconscious activities of the masses.

But the masses do not exist. Like the unhappiness they represent, they are only a reassuring dream of the human brain, a notion that evolved out of the instinctive animal brain which finds safety and identity in the herd.

In the unconscious dream of the masses, man and woman can cling to unhappiness until they die; unable to exist as individuals. In living they never really come to life; they only think they do. They live, not as individuals, but through the instinct and notion of the herd. Only the individual has the power to come to life in existence, beyond the herd. There is no hope for the herd.

The masses have no hope.

The masses always live on hope. In the modern western world, it was thought that democracy would make everybody happy. Hopefully.

The introduction of representative democracy was the first concerted attempt by unhappy people to make themselves happy. Through the democratic vote, each man could express his unhappiness by choosing an unhappy man or party to express his unhappiness for him to other unhappy parties. These unhappy parties working unhappily together would produce happiness. That was the notion. That was the hope.

Getting the vote did indeed allow the unhappy masses to express their unhappiness. But as the masses do not exist, predictably their vote has no effect. Thus men were no happier; their unhappiness no less.

Then, less than a century ago, they suddenly discovered that the other sex, the female partner in unhappiness, did not exist democratically. So they gave her unhappiness the vote too. Now everyone could express their unhappy choice and everyone would be happy — it was hoped.

But that didn't work either. Men and women were still unhappy.

So both sexes got busy. As woman tried to contribute her unhappiness to the non-existent happiness of democracy, man proudly extolled its merits to unhappy natives of other lands, who like himself, do not really exist. They were so busy working out their unhappy self-interest that they utterly failed to grasp the awful truth of what they had done.

All power comes from the people.

Through representative democracy man and woman had willingly handed over responsibility for their unhappiness, for all time. In all the thousands of years of trying to cope with unhappiness, man had never done anything so foolish or irresponsible. There had been a gradual, creeping transition towards this point, but now, with one seemingly progressive act, the individuality of man and woman disappeared into the ignorance of the masses.

Throughout the ages, violent and unhappy men had destroyed or seized possessions, tortured enemies and taken slaves. Under countless unhappy kings and tyrants, man had accepted his unhappy lot, accepted it as his own, and dealt with it in himself as best he could. He had never voluntarily given other unhappy men the right to make him unhappy. But now he had done it.

In fact, throughout his long history, man frequently died to keep that right — that extraordinary inner responsibility or power — rather than surrender it to anyone. He called it his honour or integrity. That power to him was God. In that power alone resided his individuality. And only he, the individual, could answer for it, or to it: none other than he. For this was not a notional god or good, as God or good is today. It was a living state, a being within, the being of himself; the unmistakable presence of his own rightfulness.

In those earliest of days, life as the feeling of being alive was far more vital in man. He was not the mental creature, living mostly in his head, that he is today. He possessed far less notional and theoretical information about living; far more knowledge of life (self-knowledge). He was informed from within. But over the centuries, as he slowly degenerated towards the folly of democracy and the notion that freedom could be attained through others, he became aware of a growing inner unworthiness, battling with his inner rightfulness. This was like being two opposing, living realities at the same time. And due to his more conscious state, it was more intensely real to him than we can know today.

After a long interval of further degeneration from consciousness to self-consciousness, man called this inner struggle, his 'conscience'. By then, the struggle was no longer real. Because he now lacked the inner knowledge of the one good, the struggle of his conscience was little more than a confused contest between the various notions of good and bad that others had planted in him. From a spiritual struggle deep in his vital being, it had deteriorated into an emotional struggle on the mental surface of himself.

While the struggle was still vital, man had a continuous experience of the invading force of unhappiness, the mortal in himself, literally grappling like a wrestler with his inner power, the immortal or eternal in himself. He was both combatants simultaneously, both the force and the power, and while the battle raged, did not know which would win. But he was always aware that it was a life and death struggle.

It was extremely painful at times, as though he was being killed. And yet out of that dying, when the power temporarily overwhelmed the force, came a spiritual awareness of the ineffable sweetness and beauty of life or reality within him — his integrity.

Man lived with death, within him.

Death was a constant presence; not the cessation of activity, but an extraordinary energetic activity, and when he faced it — alone, as he must face it within — he won the battle.

Death brought life! In this inner death and dying was salvation. Living with the presence of death within enabled man to know the living reality of life within — honour, integrity, living power, living God, living good. For only in the face of death are honour and integrity realised, made real as oneself.

Man and woman today have little opportunity, and even less inclination, to die for their integrity or honour, the one good, the one God within. Today they die for democracy, the god without; or some similar notion of a good or god outside themselves. The introduction of democracy marked the end of man's inner fight for life. Men and women chose to no longer live with death within. It was too painful, and inconvenient.

Death had won. And man gave up the ghost. He surrendered unconditionally to the outer good or god, the notional existence of the masses. The ghost (his false impression of himself) stepped out of his body and attached itself to a new body, the body politic, the notion that he was one of the mass of everybody. Now his power and integrity could only be expressed through force and emotion. He would have to fight for what he thought was right. Whenever he did so he would be misunderstood, bringing more unhappiness upon himself and everybody else.

Since man had abandoned the reality of himself for the dream of mass salvation, the massed unconscious now took over with its popular notions and emotions. What was popular was what mattered; not what was right. Individuality was being superseded. The chance of an individual discovering the truth and having the power to rid himself of unhappiness was enormously reduced. Such individuality was not popular. The individual within was dead.

God was dead.

The disease of death spread outwards. Life on earth was dying. The more it died, the more the disease, the masses, lived and multiplied. And the more the masses lived and multiplied, the more they killed life on earth.

All power comes from the people — as all unhappiness derives from the power of the people who have surrendered to the force.

*

The democratically elected unhappy politicians were now responsible for man and woman's unhappiness, and they did the job well. They made men and women very unhappy. And unlike any other time in the evolution of unhappiness, this time they were made unhappy indefinitely. Not even the most wicked kings and tyrants had been able to manage that. The old despots could be murdered, or when they died their inhumanities vanished with them: the King is dead, long live the King, for the new King might be compassionate and just.

Democracy did away with individuality. So now no single individual was responsible with his or her life and certainly was not responsible for the injustice and cruelty implicit and endemic in democratic society. Therefore these inhumanities would continue indefinitely. No more would the murder or death of anyone in authority, or even of many in authority, make the slightest difference. Another person or persons, similarly not responsible, would simply step in and fill the gap.

Democracy, with its injustices, cruelties and politicians, just goes on and on and on and on . . .

As democratic societies became progressively unhappy, so faceless law enforcers and upholders were needed in increasing numbers ('forces') to protect democratic society from itself. Similarly not responsible, these firm men were there to defend democratic law which, being legally arguable, is therefore unjust.

All this raises the question that nobody in a democracy, or in their right mind, dares to ask:

Someone must be responsible. But who?

The people. All power comes from the people. So surely the people must be responsible?

— No, not any more. The people handed over responsibility to the politicians.

— Then the politicians must be responsible?

— Impossible. Politicians are not responsible. Everyone knows that. Politicians don't take responsibility for the poverty, greed, dishonesty, cruelty, exploitation, crookedness and inequality which democratic systems preserve and foster. Political initiatives or an individual politician strong enough to remove the iniquities might make the people happy; but then politicians would be out of a job. So they are not responsible (except for making people more unhappy).

— Then it has to be the people who are responsible ?

— No, it can't be so. Because there are no responsible people any more. Where are they? It's not allowed.

— Then no one is responsible?

— That's right.

That's democracy and that's its invincibly popular appeal. Freedom without responsibility is the popular notion arising from the instinct of the human herd.

Under democratic rule, people thought they were happier. That was the popular notion. Increasing creature comforts and material convenience (at the expense of someone else's poverty) helped to keep the mind off the personal pain of unhappiness that just would not go away for long. But the common pay-off, the common wealth, was shared out no more justly than it ever had been.

The popular notion that justice and happiness had increased were just two more spurious arguments devised by man to compensate for his loss of contact with integrity, honour or God within. If justice and happiness were increasing then everybody must be doing well. In fact the unhappy rich (I like) got richer and the unhappy poor (I dislike) got poorer. The unhappy in-betweens multiplied marvellously; these masses, led by unhappy politicians in unhappy assemblies, stoutly maintained their position by defending both rich and poor at the same time, while doing absolutely nothing about getting rid of either.

With the superstructure of democracy creeping over the globe, the status quo of unhappiness on earth was now fixed to the end of time.

With all this distraction going on outside, man became less aware of the pain of unhappiness inside himself. And yet, as awareness of the pain diminished, so strangely, did the feeling of being alive. He was far more knowledgeable in his opinions, had an immense wealth of information in his memory, and knew what was right and wrong for the world. He also knew he was alive. That was unarguable. Yet he couldn't feel it. Which, if you look at it, is what a clever computer or robot might say.

To bolster the feeble feeling of life within him, he required more contrived excitement. And democracy did not let him down. All was provided. There was more alcohol, more fancy food; more entertainment, television, radios, music; more news and information, cars, business, holidays; and more sexual stimulation through the fantasies of films, magazines, newspapers and sex shops.

But man remained unhappy.

Unhappiness drove him deeper into material escapism to try to forget that he was unhappy. Then, adding to his burden, the awful truth gradually dawned on him. Never again could he, as an individual, do anything to stop the politicians or the democratic system from making him unhappy. No matter how much he tried to protest and publicly demonstrate his unhappiness, there was no one in authority to hear him; and no one who would do anything lasting about it. Because no one was ever responsible enough. Things only got done according to the likes and dislikes, the self-interest of the politicians (or whatever the ruling authority happened to be). The only right of protest, outside the notion of hope of it, was the ballot box every few years. But then his vote only gave some other unhappy person the right to protest on his behalf — perhaps.

Sometimes, in extreme unhappiness, he took the law into his own hands. He tried to force a particular result. Acting as an individual he tried to rectify the injustice and inequality of the system. When a man is responsible enough as an individual to take the law into his own hands, putting his freedom or life at risk, it is always in an attempt to correct or expose a fundamental wrong in society. In an effort to eliminate the gap between the rich and the poor, the privileged and underprivileged, he stole, cheated and otherwise abused his fellow man and woman.

Then quite rightly, with the full force of democracy, the blind statute of democratic law came down on him like a ton of bricks. He was beaten, humiliated, tortured, punished, locked up. The message was clear: Never interfere with ineffective democratic processes. They were designed to perpetuate the unhappiness in the system, not to eliminate it.

To eliminate unhappiness would destroy the system.

Behind all the nicely documented democratic laws, there is another highly secret, unwritten law. It is seldom discovered by anyone other than the would-be individual who breaks it. The penalty for infringement is democracy's ultimate atrocity and sham. Here it is:

— A man (or woman) who puts his life or freedom on the line by taking responsible action, and who is caught breaking the democratic laws, must on no account attempt to expose the injustice or cruelty of the system that drove him to transgress. For as soon as his disclosures become too convincing or worrying for his interrogators, he'll be declared insane, in secret if necessary, and put away without trial, drugged into submission by unhappy, faceless doctors acting in collusion with the unhappy, faceless law. And no one will be responsible.

Of course no one is responsible for this unwritten law. For, if ever the effect of it is accidentally publicised, the highest democratic authority can then confidently declare that it does not exist.

So, the man who took the law into his own hands was punished because he acted as an individual, and that was not to be tolerated. The law was there to protect him — from himself. He had to remember he could forfeit his life if he took responsible action. And anyway, responsible action would only cause more unhappiness, more irresponsibility. He should understand this now that he'd had a taste of trying to act responsibly and had been punished for it. If he must try to right wrongs, he should do it irresponsibly; act in secret, disguise himself, deceive and blame others, misrepresent himself and lie so that no one would suspect what he was up to.

He could cheat, rob, exploit, injure, defraud or steal — but he must never get caught. And the justice of this? While he gets away with his irresponsible actions, democratic society can continue to get away with its irresponsibility. This situation was quite tolerable; in fact essential.

Democratic law only punishes those who get caught.

In fact, lawbreakers are as essential to democratic society as law-enforcers. The law is only there to allow those two minorities to fight it out, providing a distraction from what is really going on. For the rest of the people it is open slather all round; a free-for-all. Take what you can get away with, and call it either healthy competition or socialism.

The Democratic Edict:
• Never forget that you willingly surrendered to politicians and their self-interest your right to be an individual. You must live with the consequences until you die. There is no escape in democracy except

91

escapism itself; but that is all provided.
- Conform to the Good and Bad that is laid down for you.
- Understand that you are a part of the masses. That the law represents the masses, the unconscious herd. That the masses must never be disturbed by responsible action.
- Get it through your head that it's forbidden for anyone to be responsible in a democratic society. Because only in that way can the masses be protected from having to face up to the unhappiness on earth.

The masses are the human ass of an irresponsible god.

The Truth of the Democratic Way of Life:
- Only the individual suffers, never the masses, because the masses don't exist except as a notion of the dreaming individual.
- By eliminating the individual until only the notion or dream of the masses itself is left, no one is left to suffer.

That is the philosophy of the democratic way of life. It is also the philosophy or truth of communism, of every dictatorship, every regime. For in the evolution of unhappiness on earth, which is the history of mankind, all systems produce the same result — the endless tyranny of unhappiness.

In the democratic way of life man discovered that he was entitled to criticise and blame others for making him unhappy. He called this new freedom 'The Freedom of Speech'. Really it was a lofty euphemism for the licence to pass the buck for his unhappiness.

Out of this crazy notion of freedom arose the quintessence of irresponsibility and misrepresentation — the modern newspaper. Here at last was the The Defender of Democracy, The Voice Of The Masses — the mouthpiece of man's irresponsibility to man.

On behalf of the masses, and in exchange for a few pence or cents a day, the newspapers indiscriminately blamed everything and everyone under the sun (except themselves) for mankind's unhappiness, without ever mentioning or pausing to perceive the cause of it. This oversight, naturally, made everyone more unhappy, including the unhappy newspaper people themselves. For newspapers, like the rest of the media, are made by people. So morning, noon and night (and with an occasional Extra!) news people chorused their unhappiness — every day more loudly and more sensationally; presenting the unhappiness in the Latest News as important and meaningful, which of course it was not. No one believed what the papers said, or agreed with it for long, because it was never the truth. What was represented changed as often as the date. (The date was usually reliable).

A daily mouthpiece to bellow the world's unhappiness gave the masses some inexpensive entertainment, without any individual having to take responsibility for the monstrous untruth of it all. There was also the notion that some sort of protest was being made. Perhaps something was being done. Something was happening . . . perhaps. But nothing was done and nothing happened that was really worth reporting, and so it continued. And all over the earth conditions representing the unhappiness of mankind continued to get worse.

Sometimes politicians, in troughs of unhappiness and egged on by the inexhaustible wailings of newspapers, sent brave young men off to war to be maimed and killed; while equally brave and unhappy women were left behind to cheer them on and weep. The politicians went on beaming, while to serve their own self-interest the newspaper people, with the stroke of a half-true report or a headline, made heroes of whom they liked; and with the detached irresponsibility of a firing squad, assassinated whomever they disliked.

God save the Queen! Or the King. But what about the people?

They didn't matter too much. No one exists for long. Which is why all the unhappy people who survived the wars or stayed behind, soon forgot those who went away and died. And they soon forgot what the wars were supposed to be about, anyway.

'To our glorious dead!'

Who?

Things on earth were going along nicely: very unhappily indeed. Remember that all power comes from the people. And all the forces of unhappiness come from the power the people have surrendered. As the people were hiding in the irresponsibility of the masses, the evolution of unhappiness continued, especially through newspapermen, hiding in the irresponsibility of their mass circulations and ratings.

The Press: licensed to fool all the people all of the time.

Democratic society now invented a new golden god and sacred idol: Freedom of the Press. This is the licence to avoid the truth every day and to blame the unhappiness of the world on everything, including death and war.

Freedom of the Press was a slogan originally invented by politicians to fool the people they were supposed to be representing. It simply meant the liberty to publish the likes and dislikes of the ruling authority without question. This authority, of course, was made up of politicians and their self-interest.

The politicians cleverly chose the word 'freedom' to imply that what was printed would be the truth. The public still believes this: 'If it's in the newspaper, it must be true' despite the quite contrary experience of most of the people who have ever been quoted by newspapers.

At first the politicians, with an assumed air of public respectability, controlled and used the newspapers by exercising the weight of their new democratic authority. But due to their obvious duplicity and stupidity, this started to wear thin. So they bribed the newspaper people to keep quiet or only mention them in a good light. They did this by revealing confidences and non-attributable secrets that had been entrusted to them. These made the headlines and of course created more unhappiness.

Dishonesty only disappears when there's no one to buy the loot.

By quietly altering (or failing to alter) legislation, the politicians managed to favour the newspapers, giving a creeping legality to their status as responsible and accountable to no one.

Now the politicians had two faces: one for the public, who did not know them; and one for the Press, who did. This led to the deceit of reporting to newsmen 'off the record', or speaking behind the public's back.

A great modern conspiracy had begun. The Government and the Press were to conspire against the people. Through the public posturing of being responsible and with the connivance of the newspapers, democratic politicians were able to institutionalise their most brilliant lie: the notion of The Public Interest.

By claiming that whatever they liked or disliked was 'in the public interest', both the newspapers and the legislators were able to protect and further their own narrow self-interests; and at the same time say they were acting in the name of the broadest, most acceptable notion — the good of all. Of course this is false, as the public good is only served when a serving individual is free of unhappiness.

Institutionalising this brilliant fiction was a consummate cover-up; the ultimate in subterfuge and skullduggery. But between them, the conspirators managed it. Everything the politicians and Press now did could be said and done 'in the public interest'. If this couldn't be proved, it couldn't be disproved either; it was a matter of opinion, or endless debate. As only the media and politicians possessed the means to broadcast their opinions, their likes and dislikes, and debate what they liked or didn't like, all went well. The public interest (the lie) was being served.

All unhappiness lies in repetition.

Previously in history, the conspiracy against the people was between the rulers and the religious leaders, the King and the Church. In order to gain emotional control of the masses, the wicked priests had institutionalised an even more seductive fabrication: the notion that a saviour — one good or God — could exist outside the individual now; that it could have some verity or true substance in the past; and that some creed, belief, priest or book was needed to find it.

The individual who lived with the presence of death and faced death within, had found his saviour and crucifixion in inner death and dying (though every notion of good and bad fought in him against this, the truth). But the wicked notions of the priests finally entered him as his conscience of good and bad, and in their unhappy worldliness, the priests corrupted him into believing that there was a saviour, a crucifixion and a resurrection outside himself.

Nevertheless, over many, many years, the authority of the priests, or the Church, being based on emotion and falsehood, inevitably lost its force and could no longer trick and delude new generations. A new form of force was needed to dupe mankind and allow history, or the evolution of unhappiness, to repeat itself. By selling their souls to the media, the politicians provided the opportunity. The ghost of unhappiness that had passed from man into the body politic, now stepped into the sensational body of media people, the unhappiest of the unhappy. And, like those before them who had surrendered their individuality to the notion of democracy, the politicians would not immediately realise what they had done — what their dishonesty and chicanery had unleashed upon the world. For nothing was to have such awful consequences. The owners of the media and their journalists seized the right to speak directly for the unhappy masses; and at the same time decide what the masses should and should not be told each day. The tricky politicians had at least had some authority from the people: but the media had no such authority. It was an outrageous usurpation of supposed democratic rights by an utterly irresponsible section of the unhappy people. These were men and women trained in habitual distortion to present the untruth as the truth and to make everyone more unhappy, including themselves.

Nothing makes man more unhappy than the untruth appearing as the truth. The only news that is new and real is the news of the cause of unhappiness and how to be rid of it. That alone is the truth. But everything on which the media feeds and thrives — the murders, robberies, rapes and wars; the opinions, vanities and problems; greed, corruption, slavery, illness, violence, death and grief — everything is an effect of unhappiness, not the cause.

To report, investigate, discuss and expose the effects of unhappiness, day in and day out, is as unreal and meaningless as saying in endless different ways that water is wet. Water is wet. And existence is unhappiness. The intelligent question is: Why is existence unhappiness? Why is water wet? And since it is an intelligent question there is no answer — only the solution. Water is wet only when you go into it or it goes into you. Wetness is not water. Wetness is an effect. Water, in fact, is life. Existence is only unhappiness when you lose yourself in it; when you serve or believe its unhappy effect; or you allow its effect, unhappiness, to enter you. Existence, in fact, is bliss.

So when it is a person's full-time occupation to misrepresent the effects as the cause, the unhappiness engendered in him or her is prodigious. In the young journalist or TV reporter the excitement of such power-without-responsibility manifests as frantic enthusiasm, and blind dedication to the propagation of the untruth as the truth. The position he or she holds is the utopia of the herd; and not given to many. But in maturity his or her unhappiness ossifies into chronic world-weariness, a sterile scepticism that comes from having seen all the effects but never the cause. Alcohol, the outer spirit, frequently provides the only relief; and for many, the only escape.

*

The Mass Media, gathering more and more power without responsibility, quickly took over as the new ruler of the world.

Originally there had been rule by man, the individual. Then kings and despots. Then democratic politicians. Now it was rule by newspapers, television, radio and magazines; a new and far more emotional, irresponsible and uncontrollable authority.

The self-interests of the newspapers, television, magazines and radio stations were paramount. The people knew almost nothing about the world except what a small minority of media people chose to tell them. 'Public opinion' was now the opinion of the few unhappy people who reported and handled the news, and the even fewer unhappy people who owned or controlled the means of disseminating it. 'Public concern' was whatever these few chose to focus their capricious attention upon, to inflate as being important. Not one person in the media was responsible or accountable. Every action, comment or report was said to be 'in the public interest'; or could be debated inconclusively with other irresponsible and unaccountable men and women.

Democracy is the Media.

The media takeover was made possible by the funk and greed of the politicians and the shameful deception they initiated and legitimised. 'Freedom of the Press in the public interest' had been repeated often enough for the hopeless masses to believe in it, and for politicians dependent on the lie of it to have to support it publicly and constitutionally.

For their infamy in selling out the people to the Press, the politicians had a terrible price to pay. Until the end of time they would be persecuted by their new masters — whether rightly or wrongly was irrelevant. Never again would the owners of the media or their journalists allow them any rest — unless they compromised or did nothing. Any politician would be privately hounded and then publicly crucified — until he sold his soul to the media again, or quit. And this could happen any day, in any democracy in the world. Especially if the politician was proposing to do some good by eliminating some of the fundamental evils of democratic society.

The lie of 'the public' was now complete.

The public is not the people. The people are the good, hidden in the corruption of the public.

Some politicians, still tricky but intuitively closer to the good of the people, glimpsed the truth of what was happening. But they were powerless to speak out. For there was only the media to speak through. And you can't ask the burglar to fetch the police.

The politicians were crooked and cowardly, or opportunistic and hypocritical, but they knew their shortcomings. They always knew what they were doing. Many of them knew there was a greater good somewhere, but none would die to find it in themselves. They settled for a secondary good; and so were forced to compromise with someone else's notion of good, and then someone else's, and someone else's . . . Until what they did, by the time they were able to do it, was hardly any good at all, and they knew it. They were doing their best in the circumstances — compromising.

The media people, however, never knew what they were doing — blind ignorance devoted to being blind and ignorant. The good was in what they were doing. They were serving the truth. They were serving the public. They believed in themselves. So they never questioned themselves or what they were doing or where they were going. There is no greater ignorance, no greater irresponsibility.

*

Sometimes in the evolution of unhappiness the army stepped in and snatched the right to rule from the unhappy politicians and the raving media. It shut up them up or shut them down. And for a while there was no unhappiness to speak of. This of course made everyone very unhappy indeed, including the army whose strength lies in never having to pretend to take responsibility for anything.

When the army tries to take responsibility for anything except force it becomes political and devious, loses its way and strength and destroys itself. When there is no power other than the army itself (inevitable when it seizes power) it becomes corrupt, political and unjust.

The force must at all times obey the power.

There is always degeneration when the force does not obey the power. That's what lies behind the whole story — the first irresponsibility followed by the people's loss of their own power; the herdal notion of the masses; the invention of democracy; the faithless politicians and the ignorant media. With the example of the army we almost come full circle. The army is force itself, the force of arms, the ultimate physical violence of the unconscious mass, the herd. So distant is the army from the truth that it actually comes close to representing the truth — life or death now, no time, no considerations, no problems, nothing in-between.

Pure force is neither just nor unjust. Force is force. It must be obeyed or the penalty is death. That's the virtue of pure force. You know exactly where you stand. There is nothing in between pure force and death, no compromise. Obey instantly; or die. No choice, no complication, no emotion. Pure force does not take prisoners; it has no consideration.

The army only loses its pure force, its real strength, when it is burdened with considerations — when it takes prisoners and has to pretend to be responsible for them. Its strength lies in not being responsible for anything except killing the enemy or forcing obedience. As soon as obedience is implicit in the numbers of prisoners taken, or there is outright victory, the army has nothing to do. Peace makes it emotional, unsure of itself, unsure of what to do next.

In peace the army's force is spent and the power of the people returns. But not for long. The prisoners (unhappy of course) are freed and absorbed into the people. The people in their unhappiness hand over power to the unhappy politicians and become the helpless masses; and the army becomes the unhappy prisoner of the politicians, pure force in the hands of corrupt force. So once again the army seizes power, in peace or war, and for a time again becomes pure force: no prisoners, no prisons, no compromise, no consideration, no discussion, no escape — just unconditional surrender, or death. But only for a while. It's only a while before the cycle is repeated.

The army can never realise that force itself is the essence of unhappiness. If it did, force would change to power. The people in the army would lay down their arms and say 'We solve nothing'. The people in politics would lay down their promises and say 'We can do nothing'. And the media people would lay down their lies of freedom and declare 'We have nothing more to say until we can say the truth'. Then the force of unhappiness, the lonely god outside man, would step back into him.

For a short time it would give him hell — but only until he regained power over it; the power to be himself, to once more be responsible and accountable with his life for the joy of life on earth.

As it is, in the dream of existence, when the army is not in charge the media through the politicians will be; and each in their cycle will give man hell until the end of time.

*

The spread of unhappiness on earth was intensified by a proliferation of telecommunication systems and by the incestuous worldwide interbreeding of the media's likes and dislikes. The beautiful earth and its people, on every continent, were objects of distress and calamity seen by an eye for profit. The nose for news smelled only the ignorance of life. The occasional report of a happy event was sure to be followed by doom, disaster, and death; with death seen as a tragedy, for the truth of death was unmentionable. And the news of the world got worse and worse and worse.

Able to cast around the whole world in an instant, the newsmen had run into a goldmine of problems and unhappiness. Never before — and this is today, while you are reading this — had there been such a diversity of unhappiness to report. Significantly, wherever the media reporters went in the world, the conditions and unhappiness there got worse. No one noticed this sufficiently to mention it or make any difference, for everyone thought the events were making the news. But it was the news making the events.

Particular events did not last long in the headlines because something more depressing, more sensational, more shocking always came in from the tireless reporters; news so bad, such a lie, that it was even more stimulating and exciting. Instant eyewitnesses, instant experts, instant seriousness, instant laughter, instant emotion, instant charity, instant everything; except the truth behind it all.

Just watch the TV News tonight.

A sign that something had gone cosmically wrong on the planet were the proliferating systems of space satellites orbiting earth. Twenty-four hours a day they provided instantaneous global communication. They should have been beaming the good news to boundless life throughout the cosmos — the knowledge that all on earth is well and on time; 'Come on in'. But the satellite systems, which symbolised man's finest technological achievement, transmitted only information, bad news, and entertainment. Information — no knowledge of any value. Entertainment — pleasure or what I like. Bad news — what I dislike; or if it's close enough to home, pain.

As the ceaseless interaction of liking and disliking, the polarities of unhappiness, got more and more intense, man's finest technical achievements poured out in a mind-boggling stream. No one person could any longer appreciate them; and certainly could not catalogue them. In spite of best intentions, they were all the product of unhappiness. And as such they caused more and more discontent.

The worst (like the best in electronics) was always yet to come. But time was no longer a protection or a barrier. Any day could be the day of the final break-through.

And so the rot went on, unabated. A continuous process, unseen and unheeded. The politicians continued their compromise and the masses remained unconscious. On no account was the massed unconsciousness to be disturbed, for to disturb it is most dangerous thing in the world. The tricky, but intuitively wise politicians always knew better than to disturb the masses, unless their massive emotion could be pointed away from home towards a distant enemy (as in the World Wars).

No one involved could see where it was all leading. Especially not the media people. They had not the slightest inkling of what was really going on. Along with fooling with masses, they fooled themselves, right to the end. Cocksure of their superficial 'good story' importance, they were too irresponsible to comprehend their role and its appalling consequences in another time. They had the feeling of being in charge, as a child might feel sitting at the controls of a great airliner while the Captain, crew and parents look on and applaud. But like the child, they could not comprehend the overall significance and responsibility of such power and position, the intelligence of which must know what it is doing and where it is going.

The way was clear for the new god of the world, the blind force of unhappiness, to do what it wanted.

*

If you are serious in the endeavour to free yourself of unhappiness you will be able to discern the truth or otherwise of this 'history'. It was written in 1985 and by the time you read it, things will have become even worse. Much that is said here has already been revealed in your own experience. But continue to observe events as they develop. Watch for signs of what is to come. Some are extremely subtle. Others grotesquely obvious.

The person of the unconscious masses will not notice anything very unusual until the final panic starts to set in. Even then the causes will not be seen and those culpable will never know what they did — for no one will be responsible.

Coming to all nations on a scale not before experienced or imagined are civil strife, economic disruption, political instability, morale-destroying assassination and public murder; terrorist mayhem, massive breakdown in democratic law and order, riots and warlike destruction of property and security; open police violence, reprisals and savage army intervention against the democratic masses.

Leading up to all this, home television screens will increasingly show unprecedented police, army and paramilitary brutality against civilian populations, all in the name of maintaining law and order.

These film-reports will be designed — unconsciously, because the media does not know what it is doing — to accustom and harden the viewers to unparalleled acts of violence yet to come against the people. The public is being surreptitiously prepared and educated to accept outrageous demonstrations of cruelty and intimidation by the democratic authorities. It will put to them that all this is normal, necessary and commendable.

If I am wrong and foolish this will not happen and is not happening. But do keep watching the television screens — without becoming inured to the violence or excusing what you see.

Civil disturbances in all countries will continue to increase against the background of mounting international distrust and fears for national survival. Along with encouraging signs of co-operation, there will be menacing re-alignments. Politicians of all nations will parley and announce agreements to raise the people's hope. But the rot will persist, nurtured by the naive media.

The bad news the media puts out will increase in exact proportion to the entertainment they broadcast. One will balance the other, so that the significance of either, or what is really happening, will not be noticeable.

Television viewers, multiplying throughout the world at about the same rate as the bad news, will be treated to an almost endless feast of human misery and wantonness — grand entertainment, like a good seat at the Coliseum on a Lions-and-Christians day.

The coverage of both news and entertainment will slowly reduce in focus, while at the same time the effect will intensify. And this will raise the emotional temperature of the masses. To see what I am saying you'll have to watch it happen as future events and as technological advances unfold.

The news will continue to be even more riveting and exciting (very bad news for someone but very exciting for everyone else). Entertainment will be coming from various hook-ups around the world and therefore appear to be happening as different events in different places around the globe. But eventually the separate events will come together and be seen as one meaningful whole. Entertainment (what I like) and bad news (what I dislike) will merge. The excitement of the bad news will become the main entertainment: no one will want to see or hear anything else. The pleasure will then become the pain, and the pain the pleasure.

Just before the end, liking and disliking will start to lose their meaning, their value. Unbridled excitement will not be far away.

Panic.

And still no one will realise the simple truth of what is happening, and how it is being done, although many will sense the approach of something unprecedented in human history.

The simple truth is that the world only exists to give you what you want: the truth, or untruth, whichever you are looking for. If you are looking for untruth — or towards the untruth as a way of life — you will find it. The more you look, and the more vigorous and determined you are, the more you will find more quickly. And so you will become much more unhappy.

This is precisely what is happening to the world and only the approach of the end of time, the end of the age, allows the individual to see this. Only then can the individual be rid of time, the unhappiness of the race. At such a time, time is intensified. It reflects its own destruction in timelessness; or lack of unhappiness.

As the world only exists to provide what is wanted — untruth or truth — the media people, like the politicians before them, have to get what they are looking for. Together with their readers, listeners and viewers, they never get enough of the excitement of unhappiness which they so avidly pursue and therefore find so plentifully in both the world and their personal lives. Were they ever to get enough of it, they would start to look for the truth. The good news would be reflected in their own lives, and in the newspapers, on radio and television; and they and the world would become happier. But of course they never get enough; they get unhappier and the news gets worse. Or, as the news gets worse, they all get unhappier.

Keep watching the media and see the truth for yourself as the world is driven towards the final crisis.

*

And so it went, to the end of time, when the media people produced the most sensational story of all time — the end of the evolution of unhappiness on earth, the end of the world itself.

There was no stopping them. As they were in charge of the emotions of the push-button world, there was no way of preventing the consequences of their ignorance. The future was theirs.

In extremes of unhappiness, and the frantic day and night search for it, the media, uncontrollable and utterly irresponsible, eventually succeeded in disturbing the masses, the massed unconsciousness.

Media lies, distortions, half-true reports and speculation inflamed the masses into a global emotional frenzy of fear and excitement; and the massed excitement drove the media into unbelievable hysteria. Everyone thought The News was the report of events; now the reports themselves became news. And the actual events even started to lag behind the latest reports of them. Media insanity engulfed the politicians. Madness started to consume the whole global society, East and West, providing the waiting armies with an excuse for the final fling of force, the final solution.

The masses had been disturbed. The sleeping giant of unhappiness was awake.

The masses represent the fundamental unconsciousness of matter, the atom itself, in which the power of creation or the annihilating force of ignorance is concealed. Once that inert and basic stability is penetrated, shattered, a catastrophic force is released. All power is in the people and the atom, and all force comes out of the power that the people and the atom have surrendered.

In the media's global society there was no distance between home and the enemy. Humanity was its own enemy. There was nowhere to go. Wherever you were was the battlefield.

Stoked with fear and expectation, the emotional frenzy of the masses became self-generating and started a fission reaction. Emotion triggered by the latest media reports created the final explosive event. The communication of nuclear missiles as the latest news was instantaneous.

It was the last news.

The final disintegrating release of force was accompanied by unprecedented natural disasters. The earth, representing the tortured human psyche, repeated the primordial convulsions that followed the original invasion of unhappiness — the psyche's conception of unhappiness at the beginning of time. Now, at the end of time, terrestrial upheavals represented the unhappiness in its death throes. And all unhappiness disappeared with the masses from the face of the earth.

Since the masses and changing face of the earth do not exist in truth, so the end of it all did not matter. The whole history of the evolution of the world was only a dream of the dreamer, lost in a notion of good outside himself.

Only the dream was shattered.

The dreamer was untouched. And freed of time, freed of the notion of unhappiness, the dreamer, the individual, awoke to the reality of timeless life on this blessed planet — the earth within himself that by the grace of almighty God is still the same as it was when he dropped off into unconsciousness, when he left the good and the truth to build an unhappy world and existence of his own.

Thank God it was only a nightmare.

He would not drop off again . . . for a while.

The Law of Life

ARE YOU BEING TRUE IN YOUR LIFE? Really being true? To yourself?

— Are you living with someone who makes you unhappy?

— Are you keeping someone who uses you and doesn't love you?

— Do you long for love; but are no longer vulnerable to love because you're frightened of being hurt?

— Do you dislike or hate your job?

— Do you ache to be free?

— Are you living with a partner you don't love and making the best of it for the sake of comfort, convenience or the children?

— Are you putting up with whatever is depressing your joy of life because you're afraid or scared of change?

If the answer is yes to any of these questions, you are not being true. You're not being true to yourself, to life. And even if things do change you won't be happy for long.

Everyone is trying to be true in their way — true to somebody, an idea of something. And it doesn't work. All it does is lead you to not being true to yourself. And that is unhappiness.

Why doesn't it work? Why can't it work? Because it is impossible to be true to anyone or anything until you are true to yourself. Then you are true to everyone and all things. And then your problems begin to disappear.

Isn't that the most extraordinary thing you've ever had put to you as a practical possibility? I'll repeat it.

When you are true to yourself, your problems vanish.

To be true you have to discover the Law of Life and start to live under it. It is sometimes called the Law of Karma. The world knows very little about this law and understands it less. The reason is that it is a conscious law, the conscious law; in fact the one and only real law. The lives of the relatively few conscious, responsible individuals on the planet are governed by it all the time. And it is available at any time to help those who are prepared to live under it and who are endeavouring to become more conscious and responsible in their lives.

The Karmic Law is practically unknown in the world because it applies or functions only in the present, now, without reference to the past. The world's laws, on the other hand, are unconscious laws; as are all the moral codes and commandments that men and women impose on themselves and each other or try to live by. Such unconscious laws are laws founded on the past, on past experience. They depend wholly on evidence or rules of the past to establish who is guilty or not guilty in the present. As it is impossible for anything in the past to be true in the present, unconscious laws are only relatively true, approximately true; and they result in compromise, trying to make the best of things in the present circumstances. The effect of these laws is to cause conflict in the person (at best the conflict of conscience) and in the world, division and discord, which we see all around us. Such unconscious laws arise from unconscious thinking, which is thinking based on good and bad and right and wrong. Good/bad and right/wrong are the world's two fundamental unconscious notions.

Almost without exception, unconscious laws and beliefs govern the lives of the entire population of the earth, the five billion persons who independently and collectively demonstrate by their daily lives that they are not yet able to be responsible for their destiny as the people of this planet, or for themselves. If you are unhappy with your life, you are avoiding responsibility for it. You are unconscious. You are obligated or considering something or someone, and you are not being true to yourself, to life.

Throw yourself on the Law of Life.

To wake up and come alive you have to throw yourself on the law of life. You have to refuse to compromise any longer with what is making you unhappy. You have to quit or separate or break with the past. You have to take action.

The action itself may well change the situation, or the other person, and end the compromise so that you can be new in yourself and continue where you are. But you must break with the old; and not allow it to bind you and blind you again.

If you are hanging on to a situation for the sake of someone else, you are deceiving yourself and achieving nothing. When you are unhappy you are not yourself and when you are not yourself you are no real good to anyone — to your job, your partner or your child. You will infect them with your unhappiness, your discontent, and they will suffer or not be themselves. You may think it doesn't show and that you are getting away with it, martyring yourself. But the fact is you are being dishonest. That sort of dishonesty doesn't rob, doesn't steal: it just spoils what should be good.

No consideration.

When you feel compelled to consider others and think you're being unselfish, you are merely considering yourself: you consider them as an extension of yourself and you do them a disservice because they are not that. If you love them you do not have to consider them. You only consider what you do not love. A mother who loves her child does not consider it. Her love knows what the child needs and she acts from there.

If breaking with someone or something makes you think it will be hard on the child you're taking with you or have to support, you are mistaken. Making do for both of you in the world may be hard on you for a while, but as long as you love the child and share your life with it in love, the child will be happy. You will be happy together. You are happy in any circumstances with the one you love who loves you. You will manage. You will get through by making the new life an adventure together. If you are being true, and not self-indulgent, vindictive or resentful, the child will understand and enjoy playing its part. But

111

above all, you will be free of the old deadening grip of compromise in your life — and you will be ready for the new.

The new always comes.

The law of life will be true to you if you are true to yourself.

Sometimes, to be true to yourself is to stay put where you are. But to be true in such a case (consciously true) means you can no longer be miserable, as you used to be. Either you will be working consciously, full-time, to make the situation right; or you will be surrendered to the situation because it can't be changed. (Surrender is the conscious acceptance of what can't be changed at this moment but may change in the next). Either way, you won't complain, doubt or become depressed because you'll know what you are doing. You'll be responsible.

When you do break with a person or situation, money can be scarce. But that will be looked after. You'll get through. Have you ever known a time when you didn't get through? Everyone gets through. Everyone has some money. All you need in the first instance is food, warmth and shelter.

Get your priorities right: don't want more than you can have now. Use what you have, what is provided. You are not going to stay where you are. You're getting free. You are not free yet. You're in the process. It is moving every day. Don't look anxiously ahead. Don't be afraid. Life will look after you in the future, if you are true now. Now is what is important. But do what you know you must. Don't lie about. Be alert. Stay as conscious as you can.

Life can't suddenly provide everything at once. It was you who strangled it while you compromised. Enough for now is enough. Trust in life. It knows what you need. And as you stick at being true life will provide what you need, more and more.

Watch the miracle unfold.

Watch life work. Watch the miracle unfold in front of you as a letter of opportunity is slipped through the door, your eye is drawn to just the right advertisement, or someone makes a casual suggestion that opens up a whole new prospect for you.

— Don't fall back into old patterns. Don't get stuck in the same situation again.

— Be vulnerable, but only to love and to what you know is right in the moment; be vulnerable to nothing else. (Learn how to tell the difference by being true to yourself.)

— Don't blame. Don't accuse.

— Don't tell your sad story. Complain as little as possible.

Be new. This is a fresh start. If you acknowledge the old by talking about it you carry it with you. Don't think about it, either. It's gone, finished. And if it turns up again in the form of a person or some other reminder, don't go along with the old emotion it excites. Pause. Hold to your newness. Be true to yourself.

The world will always be trying to drag you down, to drag you backwards, and its most powerful weapon is the past.

— Don't try to please anyone. Mother, father, family, friends. Be true. Don't give in to the tears and emotional demands of others. Yield only to love. Love does not demand; except inside yourself where it demands that you be true to the new state, the new you.

— Don't be discouraged. When you seem to lose the state and clarity of being new, don't despair,. Don't doubt or think it was all imagination. Hold the pain, the isolation, the confusion, the depression. Be the pain. Don't let it out. Feel your strength underneath. Don't think. Wait. Be patient.

— Resist trying to work out anything in the past. There's nothing to work out. You've done it; or it's happened. You've worked it out by taking action. Don't analyse. Let it be.

— Don't feel sorry for yourself. Don't look back. And don't feel sorry for others. That's backtracking. Leave it to life. Be as still as you can. The disturbance and darkness will pass. The lightness and rightness will come again.

Just hold. Be true. You are not suppressing the problem: you are dissolving it. It is the law of life in you, dealing with the weight of the past in you, reducing the old you, the old problem. You've done what you had to do by quitting, separating or breaking with the past. You did it to bring life back into your life.

The pain you feel is only the past dying, not the present. The present, the new, will not let you down.

Life will not let you down.

When you are brave and real enough to break with compromise, and you consciously throw yourself on to the law of life, you call for justice — real justice. You exert your sacred right as a human being to appeal direct to life for immediate justice. This is a right man has forgotten he possesses.

You ask to be judged immediately, now. Not whether you are guilty or not guilty (as the world will certainly judge you) but whether you are being true to yourself, true to life, in what you are doing. By your conscious action you ask direct for life's assistance.

To avoid such directness and honesty in their lives, the unconscious masses have invented the indirect ritual of praying for help. These prayers use words, thoughts and emotions as substitutes for the direct action of self-sacrifice. But only that direct action will end compromise and rid yourself and life of unhappiness.

The action of putting yourself, your life, on the line, is 'faith'. Not the popular faith of belief or supplicatory prayer; it is the faith that moves mountains — like the mountain of difficulties that seems to loom over you when you break with compromise.

The mountain is only your fear.

You are life.

Remember that life, in you, is meant to be free. And because you are being true to life, consciously taking responsibility for its happiness, you have nothing to fear. The law of life, karmic law, is not about penalties. It does not hand out punishments or exemplary deterrents. It is there for the truth, for man and woman who would be

114

true. And like the truth, its justice is extremely simple: at the man's or woman's own direct request it provides the worldly circumstances appropriate to freeing him or her from the injustice of the situation.

So, in such a crisis as I have described in which you remain conscious of the law of life, the circumstances you need to help you in the world and to help you be true, will occur. Problems will gradually or even instantly diminish.

But if you invoke the law and are not true, if you just want change, excitement, or to gain anything other than freedom from the misery of not being true to yourself, then you will attract circumstances to make you more miserable (and thus enable you to be more true). In other words, there will be more problems than there are now, or those you have now will last longer or get worse.

*

Understand that you don't have to be true in the world, only true in yourself. One is not the other; but the inner controls the outer.

The whole world of persons, of which you and I are parts, is robbing, deceiving, exploiting and misleading the people, under the guise of commerce, government, society, caring and respectability. And yet every individual inside themselves yearns to give. No one can be honest in the world for long, because everyone in the world is forced to be dishonest; is compelled to compromise; to make a deal with someone or something, for personal comfort or security. Finally, you can only be honest, true and uncompromising with yourself. That alone, that inner consciousness, will change the world.

Your destiny is to be fully responsible.

To be fully conscious and responsible for oneself is every human being's right and destiny. It means being consciously and voluntarily answerable to the karmic law every moment of your life; and living the law as your own self-knowledge.

Individuals who live the law do not try to hide from it or ignore it whenever it would suit their apparent advantage. Any transgression, they know, will have to be paid for; and they willingly watch and

115

accept life's adjudication in order that they may know themselves better, be more true to life, and more free. These men and women live and act out of the knowledge that this law is the supreme justice — the justice of being made to be oneself by oneself.

Consequently there is no feeling of being imposed on, or alienated, as occurs with the world's laws; no feeling of coercion or inferiority. This will be your experience every time you are true. The justice resides in one's own will; it is one's own law, one's own integrity, one's own self. Such men and women are both conscious and responsible — conscious of life and responsible for it. Compromise and conflict disappear from their being. And in the otherwise divided external world, the circumstances of their lives work together to serve their destiny or life-purpose.

On the other hand, to be unconscious is to be oblivious or ignorant of the presence and power of this law, as most of humanity is. Such unconscious persons are unavoidably irresponsible to the whole and in conflict with their own being. They live in a divided world of shifting values and colliding circumstances. They have no control over their destiny and no discovered life-purpose.

For such unevolved people to have to live under the simple summary justice of the karmic law, and to have to face knowingly the circumstances of their daily life as the reflection of their own inner state of truth, would be a terrifying and unjustly cruel imposition. So the eternal justice or wisdom itself protects the world and the great bulk of its population from direct knowledge of the law. The protection lies in the combined ignorance: they know nothing about the law, nor do they desire to know. They can't perceive it for themselves, and if it is explained to them they can't hear it, or they ridicule it. It does not exist for them. In their ignorance they are innocent before the law. But because of that ignorance, they are unable to be freed by it. Furthermore, they are shielded from the law's devastating implication; which I am now going to reveal to you.

To the ignorant and unconscious people of the world, this is the unbearable truth. And for everyone it is the most difficult thing in life to have to face up to.

Here it is:

As I am within, so is my life. I am responsible for it all.

— I, the individual man or woman, am responsible for all the circumstances of my life. If my circumstances are painful, I am doing it. No one is to blame but I.

— So long as I continue to pursue a divided existence, independent or ignorant of the law of life, I will feel incomplete, unfulfilled, restless and discontented.

— To the extent that I am being true to myself, present in every moment, I am controlling what happens to my person; I am being responsible, and the circumstances of my life will combine to work towards harmony, the right and the good.

— There is no fate, accident or chance which can alter my circumstances; only I, who must change them by changing myself within.

I am the circumstances of my life.

This, the unbearable truth of the law of life, as you will see, leaves you no room for self-delusion or escape — no time. Time as something that separates us from events in the past or future, is the dream, the unconsciousness, that we escape into to avoid the truth of our lives or ourselves, now. You are either true now or you are not. You cannot be true yesterday or tomorrow.

There is no 'right and wrong'.

There is only right; which is to be true, now. And there is no one or any thing to be true to — only this moment, this everlasting moment of oneself within, which is the true and the truth.

Although all the unconscious people of the earth must remain oblivious to the justice of the karmic law, they cannot escape its overall effect which is the circumstances of the world itself. Here the law, as the condition of the world, works itself out very slowly from one life-sequence, or dream, to another. That which is not faced up to in one sequence (or in any moment) must be faced up to in the next, or the next, or the next; until the truth of the law finally becomes the living truth of oneself, the being; and one awakes. This is the reality of time and existence. This is 'karma'.

All are equal, all are special.

The law of life says that no human being is more special than any other. All are equal; or alternatively, all are special; and therefore all are still equal. And yet existence shows us that all are not equal. At every level, the rich, the privileged, the sleek and the healthy enjoy a very special position not available to all. Where is the truth and justice of the law in this?

The truth, according to the law, is that every person in existence is special because every single one possesses more than some other person somewhere. The fact that some have more than others for a time is irrelevant. Even she or he who has the least, says the law, still has more than nothing, so is still special. To exist is to possess something, even if it is only a body. Less than that is to have nothing — and that is to be dead.

You get nothing for nothing.

The law of life also says that in existence you get nothing for nothing. Everything has to be paid for. Without exception, everyone must pay. Because no one is special. And without exception, everyone is paying. To be in existence, to live, is to pay. Everyone is paying today in the circumstances in their lives for what they received in the past. And what they are receiving today as other circumstances in their lives, if not already earned, will have to be paid for in the future, in time.

Thus, for everyone who comes and goes on the earth, does the supreme justice work timelessly in time. All payment due under the law of life is made in time — in time having to be spent in existence. Time is the currency of being in existence, as money is the currency of living in existence.

Whatever is owed must be paid for here on the earth, sooner or later. That payment, at any time, appears as the difficult circumstances and problems in one's life. And the ultimate payment on earth at any time is made with one's body — death.

When you call on the law of life for justice by facing up to the truth of yourself at any moment, you ask for an immediate accounting. You ask to be shown the balance between what you have received in the matter troubling you and what you have given; or between what you are paying now and what is due. You are not asking to be judged on any other matter; only this one which is your immediate problem now. You can only face up to one problem in any moment and that is always the one causing you the greatest pain or awareness now. By appealing direct to life, through being brave enough to take conscious, responsible action, you cut out time and enter the present, or the presence of the truth of yourself. And you are given an immediate assessment or reckoning. This, the balance owing either way, will soon manifest for you to observe for yourself as new circumstances in your life.

The reckoning is your life.

There is no greater justice or truth than this. It is self-evident and unerring. It is the mystery, the secret and truth that all philosophies and religions have tried to find or express.

If you are true in what you are doing, the circumstances will be helpful. But if you are not being as true as you could be — which means you are owing — you may get ill, suffer even a mild illness that normally you would not have considered significant; you may lose some money, have a fierce or exhausting emotional argument, or go through a period of severe frustration, depression or uncertainty to do with your work, partner, housing or family.

The improvements or difficulties often appear immediately. But they may also not surface for days, weeks or even months. The time-lag can be considerable. Also, for the individual starting to wake up and become more conscious, the delay can be increased by old habitual emotions that re-assert themselves and cause bouts of resentment, anger and sullen resistance to the working of the law.

Usually there is some catching up to do. After facing up to one problem you find another you've ignored. Each involves a separate accounting until you've face or accounted for them all. But the merit is that you are no longer making more problems for yourself, as normal unconscious living does; you are reducing them and renewing yourself at the same time. As you persevere, you will realise more and more that you are actually living under the law as a way of life, or as a way of love, and that its timeless, faultless justice is working in you and for you. Your life is clearer, cleaner. You are more in charge. You could never return to the old way again.

The karmic account of the father falls upon the son.

The massed population of the earth cannot be responsible for itself as you the individual can, so for the masses the karmic account runs on and on without a balance ever being struck. This is the never-never world of living on borrowed time. Its blatant disregard for the justice of who really owes whom, and who really owes what, creates the vicious injustice or imbalance that never stops growing between the poor and the rich, the handicapped and the strong, the starving and the sleek, the deprived and the privileged. So appallingly ill-balanced has it all become that only the end of time itself, which is now approaching, can settle the account. Even so, even until the end of time, it is all impeccably just.

It is all a matter of time. All are paying in time or will have to pay in time. None can escape what is due to him or her as none can be denied. Since there is no one to take responsibility for the world, or because no one is able to take responsibility for such a dreadful mass of injustice, the karmic adjustments are made automatically from one generation to another as the endless alternating pains and gains of existence. Owing to the enormous time-lag caused by the massed unconsciousness of what is happening, the debts and reimbursements due to any generation fall on other generations yet to be born. And so it is said that the sins of the fathers shall fall upon the sons.

Any immediate justice gained when isolated individuals are

responsible or true to themselves, soon disappears into the chaos and confusion of the whole — an entire world, failing to be responsible for itself, its people, its planet. Nonetheless, even in the chaos, the law dispenses its timeless chaotic justice: what is due lags behind what is paid; justice lags behind injustice; and every person without exception suffers in time.

You are the only individual.

For the masses there is no freedom from the ignorance of the world and themselves, no liberation. Only the individual can escape. You are the individual. In truth, you are the only individual. The essential characteristic of individuality is to know what is true at any time. And only you can know if you are being true in any moment.

Each individual is at a certain evolutionary point of consciousness. Consciousness is awareness of the truth of yourself or of life. Anyone able to read this book right through will have developed to a certain stage of consciousness. To a less developed person it would seem meaningless. However, as consciousness or truth cannot really vary or have degrees, when we talk of a developing consciousness in people it is more accurate to say that each individual is at a certain evolutionary stage of being less ignorant or less unconscious. Because you have read this far, because you are real and serious enough to be able to hear the truth of life, your life, you have reached a certain point of consciousness: you are now answerable to the karmic law.

You are now responsible.

As never before, you now control the circumstances of your life. How conditions unfold and affect you from now will depend increasingly on how true you are being to yourself. It is a mighty moment; one to be uplifted by.

Whatever your reaction is to what you have just read, you have no choice. You can't run away or opt out. It is already done under the law.

Like it or not, you are now responsible for yourself. And every time you perceive yourself being irresponsible, you will know it.

The law of life's eternal justice is that no one can come under its conscious control until all the implications and consequences have been explained to them; or until they perceive the truth of it through their own experience. In other words, no one is responsible under the law for what they do not know.

Knowledge is responsibility.

And now you know. Furthermore, you now have the power to help you to be true as never before, even though you may not realise it immediately. This power comes from the energy of your new self-knowledge — knowledge of the law as I have explained it. You and the law are one, although you may not know that yet, either.

Whenever you have the opportunity to be true, or more true to yourself, this energy will rise up in your consciousness to remind you. How swiftly and often you notice the reminder will depend on your diminishing inner resistance to the truth — your reducing independence or forgetfulness of the law. This independence is deeply ingrained in everyone as the ignorance and unconsciousness of the human race; until the individual is able to rise above it in himself or herself by being true every moment without effort.

From now on, if ever you are not being true to yourself, if you are aware of it and persist in it, you will automatically draw to yourself the circumstances to make you more responsible and true in that area. Invariably, these are self-corrective or painful. The justice of the law is such that in time you will actually see yourself creating difficult circumstances in yourself, or perpetuating them.

The main barrier to truth is fear, plus the desire to remain physically comfortable and emotionally secure, even though these particular conditions are constantly making you unhappy. Remember, what continues to trouble you is what you are not facing up to, what you are running from.

There is no failure.

In any situation you can do no more than your best. It is the awareness that counts — the growing consciousness of the need to be true for truth's sake and no other.

Failure does not matter. You must not dwell on the past. There will be no shortage of opportunities to try again. Life will see to that; as life will also ensure that you succeed more and more, until eventually you perceive the wonder of the law working with precision in your life and you begin the miracle of controlling circumstances as yourself.

Death, Birth and the Secret of Hell

EXISTENCE IS IGNORANCE or unconsciousness in motion. And the purpose of it is to make the individual man or woman more conscious. This is done through the karmic process of death and rebirth which, for the masses, is the unending cycle of time or existence. The individual being that you are can only ever perceive the truth of itself through ignorance, or what is false – through the person that you think you are but are not. In other words, you have to be in ignorance in person in order to emerge from ignorance as your individual conscious self or true being.

You must be clear as to what death and rebirth is and not mix it up with the popular notions that the person or masses have today. For instance, reincarnation as it is discussed and understood in the world, is a doctrinal falsehood, a reasonable attempt to give integrity to the continued existence of ignorance as a way of life.

Reincarnation is not the truth.

Reincarnation is the doctrine of ignorance playing for time in the future so that it won't have to face up to being true to life in the present.

The only death and rebirth for you, the individual, is now. This moment is your only incarnation. You can only be incarnate, in the flesh, now, as you can only be true now. You can't be true yesterday or tomorrow. You are always true or not true now.

The only death or rebirth is now.

If you quit a situation or a person in order to be true to yourself, it will be now, not tomorrow. In that moment and all the other moments of your daily life, whenever you have the opportunity to be true or not true to yourself or life, you either die (to be true) or you do not die (to be true). You either die in that moment to the person that you are, or you don't. You either die to the ignorance that you're holding on to, or compromising with as yourself, or you don't. If you die to that personal self, if you face up to the falsehood of it, you are immediately reborn, instantly freed of that part of the old person or false self that you were. If you don't die to it, you continue to live on as the same old person, the same old wearying problem that you can't escape from.

The person is the only problem.

Getting the person to the point of dying, however, is unpleasant, uncomfortable, difficult or painful, as everyone knows who has had to be brave and true and face up to themselves in a crisis. But the release, the blessed, cleansing energy that comes from being straight and new is unmistakable.

Only fear stands in the way, the fear of dying now to what you're used to.

Only fear dies.

The process of dying and rebirth is the same, whether you die psychologically, emotionally or physically. Something dies within you. It is you but it is not you.

Your attention is focused on that within. You feel the dying. You don't see it, imagine it or think about it. It is intensely though very finely agitating – disturbing, distressing, painful, not unlike the after-effects of a wasp or bee sting, or the high-pitched onset of a dose of flu. You watch without seeing, acutely aware as you endeavour to perceive: through the confusion of psychological death, through the pain of emotional death, or through the incredible palpable blackness of physical death.

At the moment of dying, the physical body which at all other times seems so unquestionably 'you', together with all notions about reincarnation or any other topic, is completely irrelevant to you; it has no reality at all.

Death is death.

There is nothing like it. Even though you die ten thousand times (as developing consciousness or evaporating ignorance must) you can't remember death. If you do, you only think you do and what you remember is still a part of a living, of holding on notionally, not death itself. In death you grow in being, not in information.

Death is always the first time. Each death is new, for death is now. Ignorance lives in the past and fears the now, the present which is death to it.

Unless you die continuously to your notional self while you are living, you will always fear death as it approaches. You will hold on. And you will be distressed, disturbed or pained in your unhappiness.

Death exists only for the living, the living ignorance that must die. When the ignorance dies, life is — and you feel and know that you are reborn.

Remember:
— In all its facets, death is the process of being made true by being made to face up to the parts of yourself that you have conveniently ignored or excused in the past.
— Death always takes place *inside* the physical body, within you where there is no physical body, only feeling, sensation or presence and there is no thought.

In the brief moment of death, even though you may still be living in the body, you are out of existence; you have overcome the world and are out of time. In that brief moment all your debts are paid.

But ignorance must repeat itself.

For reincarnation to have any meaning there has to be a 'knowing', a self that continues from one life on earth, through death, to another life on earth. No such self exists. The person you are dies with your body and is never seen or heard of again: you die along with all your assumptions of the past and the future, and all your problems, memories, fears, ambitions, likes and dislikes, wants and ideals. Your awareness, your presence (they are one and the same) survives physical death, but is never born again into another body. Only the body in ignorance of that immortal reality of your self is born. And that is not a return but a repetition, a gradual re-arising of the same ignorance which continues and will continue as long as I mistake or identify with the body as my self. When I who am the awareness, the consciousness in the body, am no longer ignorant of my true self, the re-embodiment of my ignorance ceases. I realise that as my being is pure awareness there is nothing to reincarnate, nothing to be born and nothing to die.

Ignorance begins with the notion 'I am the body'. It commences the moment my body is conceived in the womb. But the ignorance only starts to become personal, or painful, after my body is born and I perceive other bodies or objects to be separate from it, separate from what I now regard as myself. Then, during infancy my ignorance slowly develops into a knowledgeable person — I who derive all my values, knowledge and unhappiness from the erroneous identification with the body.

Would you please test this for yourself? What is your problem, your deepest worry?

Whatever it is derives from your identification with the body, your person. Because the person has no awareness of its true self or presence, which is beyond problems and death, it is ignorance personified. The person is the cause of all suffering.

The person is as unreal as the feathers of an elephant.

Like all its problems and frustrations, the person is completely false. Just as there can be no feathers on an elephant, apart from the frustrating notion of such a thing, there is no person, apart from the person's frustrating notion of himself or herself. The person is the illusion, the surmise, that grows out of the elephant, the body.

Since the person is unreal, whatever the person conceives of is as unreal and inevitably as troublesome as itself. Consequently, everything personal in existence, being unreal, perishes. That includes the body out of which the bogus person arose in the first place and without which the person and all its problems simply vanishes.

*

To make all this clearer, I am going to show you in your own experience how ignorance is conceived. I am going to take you back into the womb where it all started, where the body itself arises. For this, we won't need a psychiatrist, a hypnotist or any other kind of expert. We need only the truth, and your impersonal awareness. Anything additional will be purely the delusion of the person.

We will proceed step by step. As we do, see if you recognise the truth of what I am saying. For it is the truth of yourself. Examine every word in your own experience at that moment. Don't analyse. Just relax, read and be. And after you've read what I am going to say, read it over and over again until you start to perceive the wonder of what it all means. This will happen naturally without any effort or trying, as long as you keep reading. For what you begin to perceive or reunite with will be your true self, the eternal awareness and presence that is always there when the person, the striving, doubting problem-maker, is not.

*

It is undeniable, is it not, that you are life? And is it not true that the life you are now (not the person or the body) is already in the womb before conception and at conception? Life is in the womb in every instance before conception: without life, the womb cannot conceive.

Life is always present.

Life is present before any form of life appears. Even today you frequently have this experience of life-before-the-body, but the mind, the ignorant person, glosses over it and so it is lost.

Life, with its extraordinary quality of pure awareness, is often experienced as you wake up from sleep in the morning, before you come to realise you've got a body and before you start associating with the problems of the day. What is that awareness (which is indisputably you) before your body-consciousness, your problems, come to mind?

It is life – you – which is always present before any form of life or anybody appears (including your own body). The awareness, the life in you, is there first, fully aware.

You may think you haven't experienced this state, but now it will not be long before it happens to you. When it does, just be very still and observe it without thinking.

Let me give you another example of yourself as pure life or awareness. This occurs when you wake up with a start out of a sound sleep and for a split second don't know where you are or who you are; yet you are acutely aware of being aware, extremely alert and present. There is no knowledge of any body or any thing. Who or what is that awareness, that pure consciousness which is without knowledge or knowing, before experience rushes in?

It is life, you, before the body, before conception.

Life is being behind the body.

Where there is no life there is no awareness, no waking up, no experience, and no conception; and where there is no conception there is no body. You, life, are first – before conception, before the body and before the idea of the body's form; in short, before you come to your senses. This life, this awareness and presence which you are now behind the concept of your body, is your being.

Without realising it, you spend half your life in the fullness and completeness of this state – in dreamless sleep. Dreamless sleep, when you are your true self without any body or person, is the most consistently perfect thing in your life. Each day you seek it and look forward to it with unfailing relish. The reason you think that in dreamless sleep you are not aware and fulfillingly conscious, is because in the moment you think about it you're already awake and identified with the body and the person.

The body and the person have no direct knowledge of life itself. They are external to life. They know only forms of life (life perceived through the senses) and forms of life are not life. Life is always within. In dreamless sleep where your awareness is one with life, one with your true being, all forms have disappeared including your body and your person. Yet when you awake you still know you slept soundly.

How do you know you slept soundly if there is no awareness of being in that state? The answer, of course, is that you *do* know, don't you? It is knowledge without form – pure knowledge, self-knowledge. If anyone tried to deny that you slept soundly they would never be able to convince you, because you know it as yourself. You are aware of being, even though you can't remember it!

It's amazing, isn't it, when you look at it? By saying you slept soundly, you acknowledge having had continuous awareness of undisturbed, unconditioned being, or life. You acknowledge the indescribable continuity of the being of yourself which in your waking condition you can still actually appreciate as something real, non-existent yet undeniably positive and desirable. Deep dreamless sleep is simply the total negation and disappearance of your false identification with the body and the person. You then return to your natural awareness of the presence of life or your true self, being as you were before conception in the womb. To bring that state of dreamless sleep or preconception into your awareness while you are alive and awake is the ultimate self-knowledge – self realisation.

*

The word 'conception', as in 'to conceive', has two apparently different meanings, as you have probably noticed. One is 'to become pregnant with a baby or embryo physical body'; the other is 'to receive or be pregnant with an idea or notion'. By looking at the conception of the body in the womb, we can see how the two meanings, physical and abstract, actually describe what happens at the instant of conception.

The body is the initial object through which life comes into existence and this occurs at the moment of conception in the womb. The question is, who or what conceives the body? The womb obviously doesn't conceive; conception merely occurs there. So who or what conceives the body?

Life conceives you.

The source of all reincarnation theories and the secret behind life on earth is this: You, life, the being of pure awareness behind the womb, conceive your own body and your own existence.

You conceive your own body in or through the womb, where all life originates, by identifying with the first fertilised egg or potentially complete human form to enter your awareness. You receive this, and conceive and give life to it by identifying with it, using its incipient senses of feeling as your perception. The effort is much the same as when you look at a totally lifeless photograph of someone you love, and by identifying with the photo, you experience your love of the person, although the image has no life outside the life you are giving it.

So, in the womb you provide the embryo with your being-ness by conceiving it as the feeling of yourself; and at the same time, you give it life and identity by conceiving it as 'I' – the notion of yourself as that feeling. This is the fundamental error of human existence. From this arises all error, all ignorance.

The body you have assumed in the womb, and the equally false notion that 'I am this body', are now gestating, swelling and growing as forms of life, forms of yourself which are not yourself. Fertilisation – the bond of male and female matter – is the magnet that draws unlimited life and being into limited individual existence. Whereas your awareness was previously endless and undisturbed being, bliss without object or subject, there is now the object, a body, and the subject, 'I'.

Existence has begun for you. From now on that form and its existence are 'your life'.

*

After conception, the first sense of awareness that I the embryo have is of the utter warmth, comfort and congeniality of the womb.

Nearing the end of nine months, I am addicted to this perfection, this seemingly complete, self-sustaining feeling existence. The womb (my world) and I (my feeling body) are in almost total harmony. Body and world are one.

As I am pushed out of my mother's body at birth, this unity is violently shattered. The warmth, comfort and effortless peace of the womb vanish. I am plunged into cold space and discomfort. The change produces insecurity, unrelatedness or the first feelings of confusion, self-doubt. It is profoundly disturbing. There is the immediate sense of duality. There is I the body. And there is that which is not my body, the impinging, hostile, surrounding condition.

For the first time I am conscious of lack – lack of the warmth and comfort, the perfection inseparable from myself. I am woeful. I know longing. And gradually I know pain.

I want what I had, the past, what I was and felt in the womb, my original perception of myself as the sense of warmth, comfort and peace. I now know the feeling of frustration. I want something other than what I have or am, and I can do nothing about it. I am helpless, isolated, bewilderingly alone, incredibly lonely. My body cries. It cries for warmth and comfort, for the succour, security and enfolding presence of the moist and gentle womb. But this has gone forever.

From this moment on and for the rest of my life, I will identify with any condition able to reproduce feelings or impressions in me similar to those I knew in the womb. I will love (or name as love) anyone or anything whose presence arouses these responses in me. And my whole life will be a constant endeavour to acquire and hold on to those things and those people. In this I will always fail or be disappointed, for the only way I can have the love and union I crave is by returning to the physical womb. I will attempt to re-enter it through the brief palliative of physical sex. Then I will identify sex with love, and make yet another error. And I will go on identifying love with any condition, person or thing that provides even a degree of that sense of original warmth, peace or comfort of the womb, which I can never hope to find again outside myself.

*

After leaving the womb, my first real awareness of love is my mother. (Oh doctors and nurses delivering me to her, please embrace my body firmly with your warm skin, secure arms and good will.)

My mother's nipple in my mouth, the warmth and succour of her milk flowing into my body and the warmth and smell of her flesh outside me, provide a sense of reassurance, an incipient feeling of love, some sort of return to what I'd known. So through my strange new senses I begin to project myself further out from my body, attaching to the mother through smell, touch-feeling and taste — transient substitutes for the contentment I knew.

Could anything ever replace the effortless warmth, comfort and security of the womb, where there was no need of any object apart from myself? No. Only death perhaps. Which in my darkest misery, as I grow older in the body, I will sometimes wish for.

My new-found love or identity with my mother's body, my sense of being and belonging, is continually interrupted. I learn how to cry and when to cry; to try to bring some love into this weird, alien existence, until even crying becomes a kind of perverse comfort against the sense of loss and pain. I cry not so much out of discomfort, but for what I feel I've lost. It will always be like that from now on. So I will live this life crying and trying to bring about the impossible, to materialise what I left in the womb. As this is impossible while I think I am the body, I will never be happy or contented for long, until I die.

Such is the fate of ignorance.

*

Why does it all happen in the first place? What is the reason for existence, the cause of it? How do I, life or awareness, come to be in the womb? How is it that I, who am unlimited life or consciousness, take up such a limited position, or any position at all?

The answers are in death – behind the death of the physical body and the death of the person who dies with the body. All your fears, doubts, hopes, memories, ambitions, likes and dislikes, wants and ideals vanish and you discover the ignorance they were; that they are all substitutes for the knowledge that there is no death.

In death you lose nothing but your ignorance.

Ignorance is mortal. Death is the loss of that mortality. So in death all that survives is your presence and an awareness that is without knowledge or ignorance. I demonstrated your experience of this awareness, this pure life that you are, in the examples of dreamless sleep and waking from sleep. Now I will explain what your presence is.

While you are alive, your presence is almost totally insulated or obscured from your own and other people's experience by your body. The living body is an outer vestige of your presence. It is the past being left behind moment-to-moment and continuously mummified by your more swiftly vibrating, more timeless inner presence. It is the stuff of space and time, a living record in sense of your fleeting presence on earth. The living body registers this record as aging and finally as death.

Physical space and time are however a very small part of your existence. At death, when your consciousness is relieved of the body, its insulation, you are aware of your presence, your immortality, for the first time. The feeling of liberation is ecstatic. Persons close to you whom you leave behind may also register your presence at this time. Those who do will have no doubt, even though your dead body is lying in front of them or already disposed of, that the unseen presence is you, the unmistakable living you.

The presence is you.

Your body is never 'you' because it lags too far behind the immediacy of your presence in the body.

What does this presence consist of? At death, it is the sum total of your life just concluded. That life has not ended. It is really just beginning. At the moment of death you are filled with life, abundant with energetic presence of the life just lived. You are like a bee returning to the hive from the orchard of the earth, pollen sacks laden with living life.

Living is actually gathering. You have gathered, stored and brought with you every energetic instant of that life. You are that life. That life is your presence or self. So in death, as in your mother's womb before conception, you are life. The life in the womb was awareness alone; now it has presence in it, the presence you have gathered.

After death, the real work begins.

Although you have no perceived body, you are conscious as never before. You are a point of consciousness, from which you observe the earthly scene. Gradually that earthly perception fades. And then you pass through hell.

Hell is an energy that purges you of the residual 'hell' in yourself – emotions such as hate, and appetites deeper than those normally attached to physical consciousness and therefore not left behind with your physical body. Any pain or hell you suffer is only of your own making: what you liked too much, or disliked too much, and lost yourself in. Hell merely provides a reflection for you to perceive the attachment in yourself. The perceiving of it is the dissolution or the 'burning out' of the negative worldliness still clinging to you.

Hell is an essential part of death, a purification process before you go on. Everyone must pass through it, but not everyone suffers.

You then begin the work of life after death; which is to extract from your presence the true value of the life just lived. You do this by literally consuming yourself, dissolving yourself. You re-live that life as your new, hypersensitive, immortal consciousness, not in the shallow, lateral, A to B way lived by the old, mortal body/mind. You live it with a wondrous intensity and fullness. From every living moment of that life's seeming pain, pleasure, love and indifference, you extract the true meaning, significance and purpose. This was impossible before hell removed your condition of ignorance and innate selfishness.

You become totally absorbed in your new life and are continuously amazed by it. Three outstanding things are being done in the process.

– First, you extract the positive value of your life, distilling the whole experience into a minute, divine essence or fragrance of yourself. This is eternal or real consciousness as distinct from immortal consciousness. You are reaping all the moments in which you were true.

– Second, in a contrary, negative sense you are registering in your awareness what you now clearly see was missing from your life on earth. You note earthly experiences which in your immortal wisdom you perceive would eliminate some of your ignorance and make you more true, more real, if there was to be another chance.

– Third, the residue of your former self or life left by this continuous purifying process is forming your new immortal psychic body and life; a psychic body of consciousness in life after death, immortal but not eternal.

The order of existence is from the physical to the immortal to the eternal – three worlds. In the after death process you contribute simultaneously to each world. That is, while you are extracting the eternal essence that 'goes to' the eternal world, you are forming the negative impression that will determine your next physical life. At the same time you are automatically creating your immortal body and, through it, living your immortal life. You are not gathering experience as you did on the earth. You are actually shedding all your experience, your past, by transforming and transmuting it into relative forms of the present. In becoming less, you are becoming more – more real.

You will die unconscious if your eternal self or divine essence has not been sufficiently realised through living on earth; if your consciousness is not yet sufficiently evolved to sustain a conscious presence. In this case, you will still create an immortal body but it will be a vaguer sort of 'dreambody', something like the one you used to create to release your anxieties and frustrations in sleep on earth. Your life after death will then be a subjective dream; wonderful, but still a dream. You will be unable to step out of your own past presence, out of your own limited life or dream, into a greater presence or world of life beyond death.

*

Following life after death, the next phase is life beyond death. The world of life beyond death is an objective world; a world real in its own right and unimaginable. To participate in it you have to have a real and fully responsible body. This is 'the golden dreambody' made by your conscious presence and conscious love on earth.

The whole scheme of existence depends on what is done on earth. Only on earth is freedom from ignorance attained.

All existence is a dream.

You must understand that all existence before death and after death is a dream. It is an increasingly real dream, but still a dream. Hence the need of a dreambody.

A dreambody cannot last indefinitely. The lowest dreambody of the three worlds of existence is the physical body and it dies or dissolves very quickly. The immortal or psychic body of life after death is far more enduring. But finally, after you have dissolved yourself and used up the force of the psychic self or presence behind it, it disintegrates too, and vanishes. The most real body in existence is the golden dreambody of life beyond death.

Everyone has formed or realised a degree of the golden dreambody which is their own true self, their divinity as consciousness, the reality they are endeavouring through existence to be. It is the body or realm of the great spirits who provide, or are, the order of existence. It is eternal. It is eternity itself. It is one with God's will, God's presence (but still beneath God).

The eternal is represented by a fragrance or divine essence like a combination of smell, taste and sweetness of feeling.

The inferior immortal or psychic dreambody of life after death has an enormous range of possibilities of existence for the individual, depending on his or her state of consciousness. Like a gradient, the psychic body or psychic life extends from the most base and dense emotions, more destructive than anything encountered in the physical, to the highest, finest and most splendid examples of selfless divine love.

The immortal psychic body is represented by colour-tones. At its lowest, it is a dirty, dark brown or red. The middle range is from red to rose. The highest is yellow to gold. Gold is yellow with divine presence in it – hence 'the golden body'.

As a consciousness ascends the psychic gradient, it becomes more real, more timeless, more indefinable until finally it disappears forever into the eternal nothing, the pre-existent all that is God.

No one on earth is the highest colour all the time. Man and woman in the physical are a constantly changing flux of colour-tones from the highest, through the intermediate, to the low; responding every moment to the waves of time or past that flow through the body from the human subconscious.

Life expectancy in the immortal world can be ten times longer than is normal on earth. Time is slower or more profound because consciousness is swifter and needs less time. But the immortal body can only live or be sustained as long as any trace of the previous earthlife or old presence remains to be transformed. Immediately this raw material is exhausted the immortal life is over and the immortal body vanishes. Then, once more, you are awareness or life alone. Time has virtually ceased. You have no presence because you have used it all up. And you have no personal life to reflect off. There is nothing for your immortal consciousness to perceive.

You can only perceive what you are at any time. Had existence on earth allowed you to produce enough essence, enough golden consciousness, you would be perceiving that resplendent eternal world and be eternal. But you have dissolved or transmuted all you had in the combined existence of before and after death, and (as for most people) there was not enough reality in it. There is no need to be anxious because your essence from each life, your individual eternal consciousness, 'ascends' and remains in the eternal world. It is this you are holding on to, and reflecting off, when you are under the pressure of being true while you are alive. By the time you read this book and are able to take responsibility for your life, you can be assured that you have established a reachable divine presence or consciousness in the eternal world.

In physical death, and in emotional death in the moment of being true, you are compelled to build yourself, to make yourself. Although each life-contribution is very small, you are giving yourself a more real reflection amidst the ignorance that is every life on earth.

*

After the death of your immortal body, you have no presence at all and no one on either side of existence could recognise you. Neither can you come back into either world in any real sense of a return or reincarnation because you are nothing – nothing but indistinguishable awareness, life. As this awareness of life that you now are is universal, and is the same indistinguishable, unknowable awareness that is in everyone, there is nothing meaningful to return. Even if you did reincarnate and re-enter existence on earth, you would not remember yourself because you have no self. You might think you remember yourself in your previous life which some people do, but that would be only the memory of your past ignorance. Such memories are meaningless because ignorance has no meaning in life, only in living, where all it excites is more ignorance.

In existence, all you remember is what you are not.

Yet, after the death of your immortal body, in your particular nothingness you are not complete. It has a negative or wishful value. It contains that negative impression you registered, that minus imprint of something imagined to be an experience missing from your previous presence or life on earth. Thus your awareness is not pure nothing. You are nothing minus something, 'zero minus one'. You are a negative potential, a wish, a dream, a tale, a fantasy that has not yet been. You are life or awareness with a distinctive, negative stamp; a uniquely incomplete character. You are ignorance of life ready to exist again. This is you as pure ego. (Ego purified of self is only possible in the state before conception).

Irresistibly, your pure egoic awareness is drawn into the universal womb or chamber of existence. This is an extraordinary place. It is the ante-room of physical existence. Every human womb on earth leads here. This is where all the life that has completed the death process waits to come into existence, to enter the purely human illusion that there is some sort of fulfilment, completion or perfection to be gained in time. This notion has no reality whatever except in mankind's negative potential, his ignorance or imagination. In the universal womb, this amazing place, you wait, knowing and feeling nothing other than a subtle energetic anticipation or excitation which arises from your incompleteness. You know nothing of what is being described here (because it is described from the overview of the golden body, the eternal consciousness). Your egoic awareness is perceiving absolutely nothing. It is in an untroubled limbo. If you could know anything, which you cannot, you would know only what you are lacking; only what you are unconsciously waiting for. And you are about to find out what that is. You are going to conceive it in the flesh as your new earthlife; and then you are going to live it.

Moreover, you cannot recognise or know where you are, what this womb or chamber of all existence is. So you do not know that it is hell. You are back in hell. But this time you are not suffering because there is nothing left in you to burn. Only self suffers or burns in hell and now you have no self.

In former times there were limited concepts with which to describe the destructive intensity and incomprehensible energy or hell of human pain; when glimpsed from earth it was likened to an eternal fire, a flaming furnace or a boiling cauldron. In the imagery of the modern world the hellish nature of this energy can be compared to the first instant at the centre of an atomic explosion, or the destructively creative process inside a star.

Hell is the powerhouse of existence.

To exist on earth all life has to come out through hell, and at death all life must pass back through hell; death is the reverse of 'coming out'. The energy of hell itself is constant and unvarying, but the effect of life coming and going is radically different.

To all human life coming into existence through hell, hell is craving. On earth, the energy of hell is sex. Sex, or hell on earth, is also craving.

Hell is sex.

To the incoming life, the craving of hell is for experience, physical existence. As all human beings come into existence through sex or hell, no experience, no existence, is possible without sex, without hell.

So sex is the key to the mystery of life and hell on earth. Your negative awareness, waiting in hell before existence, seethes with hellish intensity for the sensuous experience you need. You are sexual craving itself. Together with all the other human life waiting for existence in the universal womb, you represent the one sexual desire or craving experienced by every man and woman on earth. You are no longer pure ego. You are lust – the lust for life in the flesh. You are the ultimate in selfish egoic desire, wanting to have what you want, your own physical experience. The intensity of your craving draws the earthly couples together, forces them to mate. You are their unquenchable thirst for union. The disembodied (you) draws the embodied seed back to the womb through the vagina, back towards hell, where you wait.

None can resist your fascination, in thought, feeling or action. You are unbridled sex, the insatiable, inexplicable appetite that brings shame, guilt, pain, horror and despair into the world. No one escapes you. You consider no one and nothing, neither the good, the innocent, nor the young. Fiendish, devilish is your one-pointed egoic drive that day and night sucks a river of eggs and sperm from the human bodies of the earth in coupling and masturbation. Endlessly the river flows on; but without waste, for life exists only to provide you with your endless stream of bodies. To you life's purpose is the embodied ecstasy of life giving life to itself, in the flesh, without restraint. You are the power that makes life on earth possible.

Sooner or later your egoic negativity, seething for life in the womb, perceives a positivity. There is the moment when in a particular womb the male sperm and female egg unite and bond. It occurs when both the actual and potential condition of the earth, the positive polarity, matches sufficiently the negative polarity, the circumstances you need for your life on earth. With hellish negative intensity or craving, you fix on this positive physical bond in the womb; and conceive it as yourself.

You impress your enormous, irresistible, psychic and immortal negativity onto the embryo's comparatively weak and mortal flesh, a positivity which becomes a negative of yourself filled with desire. You have physically impregnated the embryo with your missing life, your missing self — your life to be. From now on, the embryo's over-whelming negative, psychic and egoic polarity will attract to itself the positive earthly circumstance you crave. You have cloned yourself.

The weak mortal bond of the embryo frequently cannot stand the massive force or charge of your psychic negativity, and miscarriage occurs.

✳

You are the eternal contradiction. Since before conception you are the sexual craving of immortal life itself, you are the paradox of life craving for life and death at the same time: immortality craving for a fleshly form of life that will inevitably die.

As sex, you give the greatest pleasure and the greatest pain. As the hell of death, the greatest grief and the greatest release. Through sexual union and by sacrificing your immortal awareness to mortal existence, you crave the extinction of your own craving, so that you may crave and live again, to die and crave again. You are endless living and dying, endless pain and pleasure, endless past, endless karma.

You are endless life.

You are the egoic player of the immortal game played in flesh, forgetfulness, death, and in the partial awakening after death to another existence which reveals nothing but what you've already been. You are immortal. But you are not eternal. You are not uncontained, unlimited life. You are not the purity of hell itself. You are just used by hell, put through hell without ever knowing what the hell is really happening. By your craving you are bound forever to the illusory cycle of life and death existence; until the incomprehensible truth of it shines through in the reflection of your own eternal consciousness.

When this happens you are eternal. Then you see through the ego that you were. At the same time you see through hell, and no longer go through it or are touched by it. For hell in reality is none other than the eternal flame. And the eternal flame is none other than the eternal body of the eternal spirit. The apparent devilish intensity that never lets you rest is its eternal love.

Through death and craving, through one and then the other, the eternal draws you ever towards itself – uncontained, unconditioned eternal life, liberation from all ignorance.

Liberation from all existence.

Epilogue

AS YOU NOW KNOW, if you have read all the way through, this is not an ordinary book. It is energetic, spiritually energetic. (Only the spirit is energetic). It is true to its teaching. Used rightly, it will work to make you free of unhappiness. Whether or not you believe that, or believe anything in the book, is of no consequence. The book works direct, now, immediately in your subconscious, where all unhappiness is lodged.

Nothing in the book has to be remembered. What is energetic does not have to be remembered: it reminds you. So it is likely that you will be energetically reminded of your unhappiness.

If anything in the book has upset or disturbed you, it is a signal that the particular association is a hidden source of unhappiness. The more intense the disturbance, the deeper the source. You are holding on to something in yourself that makes you unhappy. The book is likely to have highlighted areas in your daily life where you are in fact unhappy, but which you are doing nothing about because you are happy to fool yourself that there's nothing really wrong. You won't like that. And if you are quick you will see that that's the point. What you don't like is what you are unhappy about, and are not facing up to.

Neither I nor the book care whether you like it or not, or whether you agree with what is in it or not. Anything you are moved to criticise will be an energetic reflection of something in your work, love, partnership or family life that you are unhappy about and avoiding: you are choosing to find the problem in the book where it is not, instead of in your life where it is. If you judged anything in the book, it was your unhappiness judging. But if you read without judgment, you will know what you have to do.

To use the book for your own liberation, you must read it again. Read it until all unhappy reactions in you have vanished. Read it over and over for the rest of your life if necessary.

Liberation or enlightenment has to be measured in something substantial and meaningful. The only substance that cannot be misinterpreted by anyone intelligent is freedom from unhappiness.

If you look at what all the prophets have said since time began you will find that their message or teaching, really applied, adds up to one thing: Live the truth and you will be free of unhappiness.

There is only one truth, there is only one teaching, and I am that. And I, the teacher and the teaching, the life and the love, am free of unhappiness now. If I am not free of unhappiness now, and now is at any time, I am not the truth, I am not the life, I am not the teacher, I am not the teaching and I am not true.

I am utterly responsible for my life, for life on earth in this body and this mind. Life on earth is beautiful and sweet. And I am here to keep it that way by being free of unhappiness.

I have been introducing you to this truth. I have shown you how to start ridding yourself of unhappiness. I have taken you step by step through the energetic process of truth which you now know as dying; and inevitably we have descended into hell.

I showed you first the mask of your personality, the obvious false self that covers up for your unhappiness; when you hear the truth of that old pretender, the mask starts to slip.

Then I confronted you with the truth of the matter; and challenged you to face the fact that life is good and that you have no right to be unhappy. Unhappiness does not lie in events or in the world but in the selfish emotion and pain that you have accumulated and continually refer to in yourself. I showed you how to handle events so that you stop gathering more unhappiness, and I demonstrated what you can do to dissolve the unhappiness that has been growing in you since childhood. Then I directed your attention to the subtle play of likes and dislikes in your psyche and the most pernicious resources of unhappiness in your subconscious. Thus far it was up to you to see the truth of what I said in your own experience, and to act on it.

However, freedom from unhappiness requires you to die to all your attachments. To even begin to do this, you have to see and realise the enormity of the unhappiness you are dealing with, at every level of yourself and existence. So I described how it all began in childhood, and showed you its end result in the world at large. I continually reminded you of the degradation of the earth and told you the whole story of unhappy existence, to drive home the message that there is no hope for this world. You have no hope. See the world for what it is; take no position; return to your place − within. And apply that understanding to the reality of your daily life, moment to moment, within and without, as your own self-knowledge.

When there has been enough dying, I know that I am responsible for the unhappiness in my life. I discover the law of life and all that follows from it. I see and wonder at the whole astonishing process of life-in-death and death-in-life. I willingly surrender to what is.

I die now − not in agony, not in pain, but in conscious life, dying to everything except what is. And in dying daily to my unhappiness, dying for life, I finally realise the incredible truth: There is no death. All that dies is my fear of dying.

Only fear dies. And the death of fear is liberation.

Information about other books, tapes, videos and seminars by Barry Long can be obtained by writing to:

The Barry Long Foundation,
BCM Box 876, London WC1N 3XX England.

The Barry Long Centre Ltd,
Box 5277, Gold Coast MC, Queensland 4217 Australia.

In North America call 1-800-497-1081.